P9-CRN-022

Doris Miller, Pearl Harbor, and the Birth of the Civil Rights Movement

Number 158
Williams-Ford Texas A&M University
Military History Series

Doris Miller

Pearl Harbor

and the Birth of the

Civil Rights Movement

Thomas W. Cutrer AND T. Michael Parrish

அ௲ௐ

TEXAS A&M UNIVERSITY PRESS
COLLEGE STATION

This paper meets the requirements of ANSI/NISO Z39.48–1992
(Permanence of Paper).
Binding materials have been chosen for durability.
Manufactured in the United States of America

Library of Congress Cataloging-in-Publication Data

Names: Cutrer, Thomas W., author. | Parrish, T. Michael, author.
Title: Doris Miller, Pearl Harbor, and the birth of the civil rights movement
  / Thomas W. Cutrer and T. Michael Parrish.
Description: First edition. | College Station: Texas A&M University Press,
  [2018] | Series: Williams-Ford Texas A&M University military history
  series; number 158
Identifiers: LCCN 2017025541 (print) | LCCN 2017028485 (ebook) | ISBN
  9781623496036 (ebook) | ISBN 9781623496029 | ISBN 9781623496029¬ (cloth: ¬
  alk. paper)
Subjects: LCSH: Miller, Doris, 1919–1943. | United States. Navy—African
  Americans—Biography. | Pearl Harbor (Hawaii), Attack on, 1941—Biography.
  | World War, 1939–1945—African Americans. | Civil rights
  movements—United States.
Classification: LCC D767.92 (ebook) | LCC D767.92 .C87 2018 (print) | DDC
  940.54/5973092 [B]—dc23
LC record available at https://lccn.loc.gov/2017025541

In nineteen hundred and forty-one
A colored mess boy manned the gun
Although he had never been trained
Had the nerves ever seen
God willing and mother wit
Gon' be called the great Dorie Miller yet
Grabbed a gun and took dead aim
Japanese bombers into fiery flame
He was aiming the Japs to fight
Fought at the poles to make things right
Fight on Dorie Miller I know you tried
Did your best for the side. . . .
I love Dorie Miller 'cause he's my race.[1]

I, Dorie Miller, brown-skinned and eyed
My heritage that of the Robesons, the Carvers, the Douglasses,
My forebears the once proud citizens of a proud Africa.
I, Dorie Miller, laid down my life
Fighting the lynch laws that threatened all mankind.
Now that my job is done, are you with me, brother?
I manned a gun that was not meant for hands like mine,
For Liberty is dearly bought and once man struggles for it
It's his who pays the bitter price.
My people are richer by those moments of battle,
Their march is ahead, their destiny inevitable.[2]

Contents

༄

A gallery of illustrations follows page 43

Preface

ര൝ൢ൬ഉ

Early on the morning of 7 December 1941, a powerfully built black messman was bringing coffee to officers' quarters aboard USS *Arizona* when bombers from the Imperial Japanese Navy attacked Pearl Harbor. The messman, a young Texan named Miller who had, he said, joined the navy to see the world, ventured, without orders, onto the battleship's bridge where he found his captain, Mervyn Sharp Bennion, lying mortally wounded. Miller assured his dying commander that "You've trained us well, Captain," and held him in his arms until he died. The young messman then made his way to an unmanned antiaircraft gun where, in a righteous fury, he began to shoot down Japanese torpedo bombers.

At least that is the way that the 2001 film *Pearl Harbor*, featuring Cuba Gooding Jr. in the role of the heroic messman, told the tale. But, as *Time Magazine* film critic Jess Cagle wrote of the movie, it "reaches for historical accuracy—at least until it gets in the way of the main story." The depiction of Doris Miller is a case in point. For instance, he served aboard the battleship *West Virginia*, not *Arizona*. Captain Bennion did not die in his arms, and in all likelihood, Messman Miller shot down no Japanese planes.[3] And, earlier in the film, his highly improbable conversation with a sympathetic young white nurse would have been entirely taboo at that time and place, as evidenced by the encounter between a black man and a white woman fourteen years later in Money, Mississippi, that precipitated the brutal lynching of Emmitt Till. As James Jackson Kilpatrick, editor of the conservative *Richmond News Leader*, wrote in his 1962 defense of traditional Southern racial mores, *The Southern Case for School Segregation*, "White infants learn to feel invisible fences as they crawl, to sense unwritten boundaries as they walk. And I know this much, that Negro children are brought up to sense these boundaries, too."[4] The movie's depiction of this brief interracial encounter, however innocent, portrays a mood of familiarity and consideration in which a young black man brought up in the Jim Crow South would have indulged only at the risk of his life.

In fact, the true story of Doris Miller is less heroic than depicted in Hollywood's version of his deeds on that infamous December morning. He did not, in all probability, shoot down any of the attacking Japanese airplanes. At the same time, however, it is far more so, as his was a fight not only against a foreign enemy but, at least equally significantly, a battle against racial prejudice in the US Navy, in his native Texas, and in the general American culture besides. Moreover, his struggle is much more complex than the film would have it, with implications reaching far beyond those of a black sailor seeking revenge for his stricken captain and his stricken ship. His contribution to his country was powerful and permanent.

—ᨆ—

Doris Miller was an improbable American hero. The son of black sharecroppers and the grandson of former slaves, he was born into rural Central Texas, one of the most racially prejudiced regions of the country, in America's most racially violent era. Moreover, he came of age in the midst of the Great Depression, dropping out of high school as a teenager in order to earn enough money to enable his family to survive. Joining the US Navy, he was relegated—as were all men of his race—to the lowly messman's branch, where his only opportunity was to wait on white officers.

But at Pearl Harbor, 7 December 1941, he stepped onto the bridge of his ship, the USS *West Virginia*, where he moved his mortally wounded captain to a place of greater safety and then manned a Browning .50-caliber machine gun, a weapon in which he—in common with all of his fellow messmen—had no training. Nevertheless, in spite of constant bombing and strafing from Japanese aircraft, he continued firing at the swarming dive bombers and torpedo planes until he was out of ammunition and ordered to abandon the sinking ship. Even then, Miller pulled uncounted numbers of wounded sailors from the flaming waters of the devastated "Battleship Row."

Despite the navy's attempts to suppress the story of his heroic activity, Miller's story came to light, and the African American press quickly made him not only the first American hero of World War II, but also the most celebrated black man in uniform. In light of its policy of racial segregation and denial of black sailors any berth or rating other than that of servant, the navy would have preferred that he remain unheard of, but under pressure from the black community and politicians eager for the black vote, it awarded Miller the Navy Cross, making him the first black sailor ever so decorated.

This self-effacing Texas sailor quickly overtook even the formidable Joe Louis as black America's favorite hero and became the navy's spokesman in the black community as well as the first African American sent on a public speaking tour or a bond drive by America's armed forces. After a highly publicized tour through a number of US cities, Miller returned to active duty. Assigned to the escort aircraft carrier *Liscome Bay*, he was killed in action on 23 November 1943 when the ship was torpedoed and sunk, taking down 53 officers and 591 others in the greatest loss of life ever suffered aboard a single ship in US naval history.

Miller left few tangible traces of his brief life. His boyhood home in McLennan County was inundated when the Bosque River was dammed in 1965 to form Lake Waco, and his family's new home in Waco was destroyed by fire in 1957, taking his medals and his small file of correspondence. But the memory of his life has burned strong as a paradigm of how an underprivileged and oppressed young man from rural Texas could rise above poverty and racial

discrimination to display exemplary courage, devotion, and patriotism despite the challenges of living in a culture that sought only
to exploit him and hold him in subjugation.

Songs and poems have been written about him; monuments
have been erected in his honor; streets, buildings, and neighbor-
hoods bear his name; the navy named a ship for him; he has been
represented in major motion pictures; and since 1941 supporters
ranging from friends and family members to the US Congress
have sought the Congressional Medal of Honor for him.

But far more significantly, Doris Miller's actions at Pearl Harbor,
and the legend that they engendered, were directly responsible for
helping to roll back the navy's unrelenting policy of racial segregation and prejudice and, in the process, helped to launch the civil
rights movement of the 1960s that brought a legal end to the worst
of America's racial intolerance.

Acknowledgments

๏

W e offer sincere thanks to the following friends and colleagues for their valuable help and support: Thomas L. Charlton (Fort Worth, Texas); Geoff Hunt, Paul Fisher, Amie Oliver, and John Wilson (Baylor Texas Collection); Timothy Grundmeier, Joel Iliff, and Thomas Tacoma (Baylor History Department); Gerald R. Powell (Baylor Law School); Doreen Ravenscroft (Waco Cultural Arts Fest); Hon. Chet Edwards (McLean, Virginia, and Waco, Texas); Bertha Sadler Means (Austin, Texas); Betty Shankle, Karen L. Hopkins, and Beverly J. Carver (Special Collections, University of Texas at Arlington Libraries).

Thanks also to Shannon Davies, Jay Dew, Katie Duelm, and Alison Tartt of the Texas A&M University Press for their invaluable encouragement and assistance.

Doris Miller,
Pearl Harbor, and
the Birth of the
Civil Rights Movement

1

"Seagoing Bellhops, Chambermaids, and Dishwashers"

Black Sailors in a White Navy

ᏱᎥᎥᎥᏬ

Nothing else made Negro citizenship conceivable,
but the record of the Negro as a fighter.

—W. E. B. Du Bois, *Black Reconstruction in America*

With the outbreak of the Civil War, former slave and great Abolitionist Frederick Douglass "urged every man who could to enlist to get an eagle on his button, a musket on his shoulder, and the star-spangled banner over his head." Military service, he believed, would bring not only freedom for enslaved African Americans but equal rights under the law to those who had defended the Union.[1]

Near the end of World War I, William Edward Burghardt Du Bois, editor of the National Association for the Advancement of Colored People's magazine, *The Crisis,* and the most talented black writer of his generation, published an editorial avowing that "we of the colored race have no ordinary interest in the outcome. That which the German power represents today spells death to the aspirations of Negro[e]s and all the darker races for equality, freedom, and democracy. Let us not hesitate. Let us, while this war lasts, forget our special grievances and close our ranks shoulder to shoulder with our white fellow citizens and the Allied nations that are fighting for democracy."[2]

Fighting for one's country has long been one of the markers of citizenship, but since full citizenship for African Americans has always been problematic for the white majority, black servicemen were either not welcome in America's armed forces or grudgingly included to serve in menial functions and when manpower needs were dire.

The tradition of black sailors in the US Navy was, by 1942, a long and honorable one. They had served in the navy during every one of its wars and were a particularly vital source of manpower for the Union Navy during the American Civil War. During the American Revolutionary War, highly skilled black mariners served in the Continental Navy as well as aboard state-sponsored navies, privateers, and merchant ships. With American independence in 1783, however, and the demise of the Continental Navy, most black sailors returned to the bondage of slavery.

When the United States reconstituted its navy in 1794 to defend its merchant vessels against attacks by Barbary pirates, free blacks were allowed to enlist with the permission of the commanding officer. The navy, however, severely restricted the numbers of African Americans who might serve, with the acting secretary of the navy, Isaac Chauncey, proscribing a limit of 5 percent on the number of black recruits that the service might enlist. This quota system continued for the remainder of the antebellum period.

During the War of 1812—largely a naval war—African Americans again volunteered their services. They made up approximately one sixth of the total naval personnel and were found aboard US naval vessels in all ratings. Capt. Isaac Chauncey wrote to Oliver Hazard Perry that "I have yet to learn that the color of the skin, or the cut and trimmings of the coat, can affect a man's qualification or usefulness. I have nearly 50 blacks aboard the ship, and many of them are among my best men."[3] John Johnson, a black sailor aboard the US privateer *Governor Tompkins*, was mortally wounded in an engagement with a British frigate. For his courage and spirit, his captain, Nathaniel Shaler, wrote to a fellow officer, he "ought to be registered in a book of fame and remembered with reverence as long as bravery is considered a virtue."[4] Upshur Parsons, surgeon of the USS *Guerriere* under Commodore Thomas McDonough, noted that "there seems to have been an entire absence of prejudice against the blacks as messmates among the crew."[5]

African Americans proved especially vital in the navy during the Civil War. By the eve of the war, black sailors made up approximately 2.5 percent of the naval enlisted force. The wartime requirement for additional manpower, however, forced the navy to abolish its 5 percent quota, and the service actively recruited free black men, many of whom had developed maritime skills while working on fishing boats and coastal and riverine commercial vessels. By September 1861 the Navy Department had authorized the enlistment of black sailors "when their services can be made useful under the same forms and regulations applying to other enlistments," and on 17 July 1862, Congress authorized President Abraham Lincoln to employ "persons of African descent" as he saw fit to help preserve the Union.[6]

Black sailors were to receive the same pay, clothing, food, medical attention, and job opportunities as their white shipmates. With the 5 percent quota system removed, hundreds of free blacks enlisted. Moreover, as escaped slaves by the hundreds sought refuge with the Union Navy, Secretary of the Navy Gideon Welles authorized the active recruitment of runaway slaves for naval service. In May 1863 he announced that "the large number of persons known as contrabands flocking to the protection of the United States flag affords an opportunity to provide in every department of the ship, especially for boats crews, acclimated labor." Flag officers were instructed to enlist them freely. At the end of June, Secretary Welles called Adm. David G. Farragut's attention to newspaper reports that near Brashear City, Louisiana, more than 7,000 black people were being fed at government expense, and inquired whether some of the able-bodied men could be enlisted for naval service,[7] and instructed David Farragut of the East Gulf Blockading Squadron to expedite the recruitment of "contrabands" since "enlistments do not keep pace with the wants of the service." The navy's decision to enlist self-liberated slaves enabled ships to remain on blockading station and conduct combined operations on the western rivers.[8] This experience provided evidence that "a large scale racial integration was not only feasible, but practical," and by the end the war, 23,000 black sailors made up approximately 20 percent of the crews in the Union Navy.[9]

Robert Blake, an escaped slave, became the first black sailor to receive the Congressional Medal of Honor. Blake served aboard the gunboat USS *Marblehead* and was awarded the medal on 16 April 1864 for his service during an engagement with Confederate shore batteries on Christmas Day, 1863.[10]

The experience of black sailors was not, however, without its negative aspects. Despite the navy's success in utilizing them on a large scale, on 18 December 1863 Welles established a new policy declaring that "contraband" wages were to be limited to ten dollars a month and that they were not to be enlisted with any higher rating than landsman. "If found qualified after being shipped," however, Welles allowed that they "may be advanced by the commanding officer of the vessel in which they served to the rating of seaman."[11]

Worse, with so many black men enlisting—one estimate claims that as many as 15 percent of all sailors in the Union Navy were former slaves—white sailors, reflecting the attitudes of the society from which they came, began to resent African Americans and blamed the war on them as a group. Cases of forced segregation, verbal abuse, and fighting were not uncommon, and in a general order to the Mississippi Squadron in 1863, Acting R. Adm. David Dixon Porter barred blacks from becoming petty officers and directed his officers to have them live and mess separately from the white sailors. Such examples of discriminatory practices evoked disharmony aboard ship, and black sailors were, in too many cases, mistreated to the point that some deserted from the naval service.[12]

Despite such blatant racial prejudice, during the Civil War African American sailors filled a wide variety of enlisted ratings, served in every enlisted billet on every type of ship in the navy, and served in every theater of the naval war. But, with the end of Reconstruction, the black citizen's relationship with the navy badly deteriorated.[13]

In the decades following the Civil War, discrimination and the rise of Jim Crow laws increased, the number of black sailors serving in the navy steadily declined, and although several young black men had been admitted to the US Naval Academy at Annapolis during the Reconstruction era, none were graduated. Black sailors lost the status that they had earned with wartime service, and their participation in the fleet dropped from a high of 20 percent in 1865 to 13.1 percent in 1870, and by the 1890s only 9.5 percent of the enlisted force was black. During the Spanish American War, the navy enlisted blacks into the ranks on a fully integrated basis. It did, however, limit African Americans to the enlisted ranks.

Following the Supreme Court's 1896 *Plessey v. Ferguson* decision to legalize segregation, the number of black sailors declined even further, such that by the beginning of World War I blacks made up less than 3 percent of enlisted men. Further, segregation was rapidly becoming a part of naval policy, a reflection of national social patterns. During the administration of Woodrow Wilson—a native Georgian—the navy reduced the number of black enlistments, and Secretary of the Navy Josephus Daniels of North Carolina continued the practice of barring black recruits from serving in combat ratings. Of the 10,000 African Americans in the navy during his tenure, all but a few were assigned to the messman branch, where they worked in the laundries and galleys and served at the officers' mess and maintained the officers' billets aboard ship.

Segregation was deemed necessary because of what white Americans saw as the inherent criminality of African Americans. A number of pseudo-scientific studies—including one conducted by the Army War College as late as 1940—described the African American as having "less developed mental capacities" and concluded that blacks were physically unfit for combat duty because their brains were smaller than those of whites.[14] Secretary of War Henry L. Stimson noted in his diary that "leadership is not imbedded in the Negro race. To try to make commissioned officers to lead them in battle," wrote this native New Yorker, "is only to work a disaster to both. Colored men do very well under white officers but every time we try to lift them a little beyond where they can go, disaster and confusion follows."[15] Thus, not only did the navy maintain that blacks were capable of performing only menial duties, but consigning them to servant status also made it easier to segregate the races aboard ship.[16]

Nevertheless, nearly 300,000 black men served in the US Army and Navy during World War I. Despite the military's low opinion of them, African Americans fought bravely and well, and they expected white America to acknowledge their service with loosened restrictions and the death of Jim Crow. "We return from fighting," wrote W. E. B. Du Bois. "We return fighting. Make way for Democracy! We saved it in France, and by the great Jehovah, we will save it in the United States of America."[17]

But with the end of the war, black veterans faced a country driven to madness by racism. Schools and public bathrooms and drinking fountains remained segregated, and the number of lynchings increased. As Charles Hamilton Houston, formerly a first lieutenant in the 368th US Infantry, a veteran of the war in France, and later a leading attorney for the NAACP, observed bitterly, "The hate and scorn showered on us Negro officers by our fellow Americans convinced me that there was no sense in my dying for a world ruled by them. I made up my mind if I got through this war I would study law and use my time fighting for those who could not strike back."[18]

Waco's black veterans marched in the city's Armistice Day parade, held on 11 November 1918, along with the A. J. Moore High School Band, black Boy Scout troops in uniform, and members of the Negro Chamber of Commerce and groups of African American civilian defense workers, air raid wardens, auxiliary firemen, auxiliary policemen, and ambulance drivers.[19] But 1919 was a year of violence and upheaval, too often triggered by the sight of black veterans returning in uniform. Those veterans witnessed the Ku Klux Klan marching in Washington, DC, and found segregation undiminished.

Lynchings greatly increased in the South, and race riots infested the North. Southern whites—frightened by the specter of thousands of black men with ideas and experiences of social equality gained from their overseas service as well as combat experience—made every effort to maintain their old policy of black subordination. In the "Red Summer" of 1919, seventy-seven blacks were lynched. Of those victims, ten were veterans, murdered while still in uniform.[20]

After 4 August 1919, the navy accepted no new black enlistees, ensuring an all-white navy in the future. Further, in 1922, under the administration of President Warren G. Harding, naval officials determined that white sailors should not be forced to take orders from black personnel. The solution was to remove African Americans from petty officer status. By 1932 only 441 black men out of a force of 81,120—barely one half of one percent of the enlisted force—served in the navy.[21] A full quarter of those men served as messmen, and—because officers thought Filipinos made better servants—even the messman's branch was closed to recruits. Not until December 1932, when the Philippines gained independence from the United States, did the anticipated shortage of Filipinos cause the navy to again enlist black messmen. "You have to understand that when Franklin Delano Roosevelt was president in 1932, he opened up the Navy again to blacks, but in one area only; they were called mess attendants, stewards, and cooks," said Clark

Simmons, who was a mess attendant on the USS *Utah* during the
Pearl Harbor attack. "The Navy was so structured that if you were
black, this was what they had you do in the Navy—you only could
be a servant."[22]

By 1939 the numbers of black sailors had reached only 2,400,[23]
but when, in October 1940, in anticipation of the coming of World
War II, the Selective Service Law was passed, the War Department
announced that black personnel were to be conscripted in the
same proportion as in the general population. Blacks and whites,
however, would serve in racially segregated units commanded by
white officers. According to Secretary of War Stimson, the draft
was prepared to "give the Negro[e]s a fair shot in every service,
even in aviation where I doubt very much they will not produce
disaster there. Nevertheless, they are going to have a try but I hope
for heaven's sake they don't mix the white and colored troops together in the same units for then we shall certainly have trouble."[24]

Secretary of the Navy William Franklin Knox, moreover, declared that "the enlistment of Negro[e]s leads to disruptive and
undermining conditions," and that blacks, therefore, could be
accepted in no other capacity than as mess attendants. According to the Department of the Navy, "The policy of not enlisting
men of the colored race for any branch of the naval service but
the messman's branch was adopted to meet the best interests of
general ship efficiency." This policy it claimed, served not only
the best interests of the navy, but "the best interests of [African
Americans] themselves," as well.[25]

The Crisis, the magazine of the NAACP, responded in September 1940: "We hope American Negro citizens appreciate fully what
this policy means to them." More was involved in naval service, it
maintained, "than standing on the deck of a warship in a white
uniform. To be stigmatized by being denied the opportunity of
serving one's country in full combat service in the Navy is humil-
iating enough. But the real danger and greater injustice is to deny
a tenth of the citizens of this country any benefit whatsoever from

the billions of dollars spent on our Navy. . . . At the same time we're supposed to be able to appreciate what our white fellow citizens declare to be the 'vast difference' between American democracy and Hitlerism."[26]

The same month that the Selective Service Law was passed—October 1940, one year after Doris Miller had joined the navy—fifteen black messmen from the cruiser *Philadelphia* voiced their discontent in a letter published by the influential black newspaper, the *Pittsburgh Courier*.[27] Describing themselves as "seagoing bellhops, chambermaids and dishwashers," they complained that "with three months of training in making beds, shining shoes and servicing officers completed we are sent to various ships and stations of the Navy. The white sailor after his training period is not only eligible for the branch of service he has chosen but he is automatically advanced in ratings and his pay is increased to $36.00 a month without ever having to take an examination." In contrast, they said, black sailors were required to serve a full year at $21.00 a month and then pass a test, which still did not guarantee them a rating.[28]

The navy's response was to issue dishonorable discharges to two of the sailors and undesirable discharges to the remaining thirteen. To America's black community, however, the "*Philadelphia* Fifteen" were not troublemakers but heroes, "unjustly penalized for demanding their manhood rights."[29]

In view of such mistreatment of black sailors, one year before the attack on Pearl Harbor the *Pittsburgh Courier* was convinced that if war came, blacks would not be allowed to fight: "The war department and the navy department plans for the coming war to DEGRADE you. They would make war without you if they could." This was, according to the *Courier*, a "challenge to your right to citizenship."[30]

President Roosevelt, unwilling to antagonize a Congress dominated by the Southern Democrats, did, in fact, seek to maintain the racial status quo, endorsing the armed services' policy of strict racial segregation. But the outbreak of war in Europe and the president's characterization of the Western democracies as defenders of the Four Freedoms roused the nation's conscience.

Thus, after years of supporting the New Deal's liberal social welfare agenda, many progressive newspapers began to challenge what they perceived as presidential hypocrisy. In response to the public clamor for change—prompted as it was by Doris Miller's story and by the president's characterization of the Western democracies as morally superior defenders of the Four Freedoms—by January 1942, Roosevelt had begun to alter his policy. He attempted to placate African Americans with token "experimental" opportunities in military training and service that were separate but never equal.

2

"Going Nowhere"

Depression-Era McLennan County

oris Miller, the grandchild of slaves, was born near Erath, Texas, in the farming community of Willow Grove, some eight miles northwest of Waco, on Columbus Day, 12 October 1919, the third child of Connery and Henrietta Miller.[1]

Several stories as to why this baby boy was given a "girl's name" have been passed down. His younger brother, Arthur, later said that "sometimes couples want girls after they already have a string of boys. I'm not saying that's the reason, but that's the closest I can come to." But the most convincing is that the midwife who assisted at his birth was positive that the baby would be a girl. She liked the name, and knowing that his mother wanted a girl, bestowed it upon him before he was born. "She waited on me and she wanted to name him and she just named him Doris," said Henrietta Miller in a 1979 interview.[2]

The Miller family lived in a three-room sharecropper's cabin—a kitchen; a living room, where the boys' parents slept; and a bedroom for the four boys. "This didn't leave much privacy," Arthur later recalled, "but then we didn't stay in the house much." The Miller family farmed the twenty-eight acres surrounding their home, primarily growing cotton, but supplementing that cash crop with corn, beans, and squash as well as chickens, cows, and hogs for subsistence.[3] "I imagine he ate beans and cornbread," said his boyhood friend Ray Burks. "He was just a common young man. He was raised up on the farm, chopped cotton and that sort of thing."[4]

Waco, located at the confluence of the Brazos and Bosque Rivers, was the rapidly growing metropolis of an extensive cotton-growing region of blackland prairie, with a population of approximately 40,000 and boasting seventeen public schools (four of which served black children), sixty-nine saloons, and sixty-three churches. William Cowper Brann, the irrepressible editor of a notorious Waco weekly, the *Iconoclast*, noted that the city's streets were so smooth and even that "a mountain goat can traverse them with comparative ease" and that they were so clean that "it is seldom that a mule gets lost in the mud." But more chilling was his only half-ironic observation that within the city limits grew a tree "on which 37 men have been hanged." That tree, he maintained, "is now regarded with a species of awe by the younger natives."[5]

In the years during and immediately following World War I, McLennan County—located along the cultural fault line where the Old South meets the Wild West—was a notorious bastion of Ku Klux Klan activity. In 1915—a year in which the boll weevil exacerbated already explosive racial tensions by threatening to devour the county's cotton crop—David Wark Griffith's *Birth of a Nation* was first shown in Waco. The *Waco Times Herald*'s review of the grotesque masterpiece proclaimed the paper's satisfaction that, as depicted in the film, when black freedmen attempted to claim their place in Southern social and political life, "an army of men," the Klan, "whose work was swift, sure and silent . . . visited stern justice on the despoilers of their homes, and fought only that the superiority of the white race might prevail." This review echoed an editorial from the neighboring *Temple Daily Telegram*, following a particularly horrifying lynching in that town on 29 July 1915: "When the white mother lies down with her babies at night in the country home . . . she knows that, whatever the power of the law, she may put her trust in a manhood whose vengeance is quick and terrible." Doris Miller was born only three years after Jesse Washington had been lynched near the McLennan County courthouse. In what came to be known as "the Waco Horror," on 15 May 1916 the seventeen-year-old Washington was beaten, stabbed, mutilated, hanged, and burned by a white mob of from ten to fifteen thousand while Mayor John Dollins and Chief of Police Guy McNamara looked on in complacent satisfaction. So virulent was the white animosity toward blacks in McLennan County that Brann of the *Iconoclast* suggested that "if the South is ever to rid herself of the rape-fiend she must take a day off and kill every member of the accursed race that declines to leave the country." Racism, the birth defect of this country, remained a lasting legacy.[6]

The third of four sons, Doris Miller learned early to help around the house, cook meals, and do laundry as well as work on the family farm. According to Connery Miller, his son was "a good boy who never gave anybody any trouble." When not in the fields or at school, according to a Speegleville neighbor, Doris and Selvia would play a rough-and-tumble variation of baseball called "one-eyed-cat" (also called "one old cat" or "one-o'-cat"), using wooden boards for bats and wound-up string for a ball. Yet his mother was to tell a journalist in 1943 that, although "Doris was always a very good boy," he was also "a coward," and she "had to spank him very often to make him protect himself."[7]

Miller attended primary school, first at Kimmonsville and then at Willow Grove in rural McLennan County, but he never began the academic year until the cotton had been harvested. As his mother later informed a Waco journalist, "times were rough when the boys were small, but the family managed to stay out of the soup lines with the crops they raised." The Miller boys often missed the first days of the school year while helping their father in the fields, but, Mrs. Miller insisted, "they always managed to catch up and stay in school."[8]

In fact, Miller received much of his education, guidance, and world perspective from the leadership at his church, the New Hope Baptist, one of the oldest African American churches in Waco.[9] After finishing grade school, the teenage Miller attended A. J. Moore High School at the corner of Clay and River Streets, Waco's first public school for African Americans. He was a lackluster student, but at 6 feet 3 inches tall and weighing 225 pounds, he was a left-handed pitcher on the school's baseball team and an outstanding fullback on the football team. He was said to have inherited his size and strength from his father, Connery Miller. According to family lore, upon being told in a Sunday School class that Sampson was the strongest man in the world, one young student corrected the teacher: "No," he said, "Connery Miller was the strongest man ever to live."[10]

Boyhood friend George Burks recalled that Doris Miller—known then to his friends as "Power," presumably because he was bigger than they—was "a nice fellow."[11] Another classmate, Bertha Sanders Means of Austin, remembered Miller as "such a nice person. I think he was a model student. He was just a cute little youngster who minded his own business."[12] And another, Pauline Adams, agreed: "He was a real sweet person, not rowdy like the other boys. He was quiet and unconcerned and didn't talk too much,"[13] but Jeffery Gipson, who went on to become a professor of chemistry at Virginia Union University in Richmond, remembered Miller as "just as talkative as either of us."[14] All were astounded that so quiet and polite a young man would become a military hero.

Failing to pass the eighth grade, Miller applied to join the Civilian Conservation Corps but was not accepted because his family was not on public relief. Therefore, he started school again on 25 January 1937 at age seventeen, but by 30 May 1938 he had decided to drop out in order to assist his financially strapped family through the worst years of the Great Depression. "We were kinda hungry in those days," his mother later recalled. "He wanted to help out."[15]

Oscar Reese, who grew up with Miller in the community of Willow Grove, recalled that for a time he supplemented the family income by working as a cook in a small restaurant in downtown Waco. "He thought that he could not make enough money to help his family survive, so he decided to join the Navy." When not at work, he filled his time fishing and squirrel hunting with his father's single-shot .22 rifle in the woods and fields along the nearby Bosque River and completing a correspondence course in taxidermy. "But he didn't get any money in that," said Leroy Ramsey; "it just didn't work out," so he decided to go into the service.[16]

Before reaching his eighteenth birthday, Miller attempted to enlist in the US Army; his father, who, according to a neighbor "did not want the family to be split up," refused to sign the required consent forms. But on 16 September 1939, to see the world and earn some money to send home, he enlisted for a six-year tour of duty in the US Navy at its Dallas recruiting station. The only berths that the navy then offered to black recruits were in the messman branch, but "it beats sitting around Waco working as a busboy, going nowhere," Miller was quoted as saying.[17]

After two weeks at home with his family, Doris Miller was aboard the segregated Santa Fe Railroad "Super Chief," traveling east for twelve weeks of recruit training in Virginia. The "boot camp" was located in the "B" section of the Norfolk Naval Base and hence came to be known as "Unit B–East." There black recruits took part in regular boot camp routine—but were strictly segregated. They were scheduled "a special time to go to the swimming pool or wherever, so we wouldn't be mixed with the white recruits," Miller's friend and classmate Thomas Mouzon later recalled. They learned their battle stations, which were in the magazines serving only as ammunition handlers. Their commanding officer at Norfolk was, of course, white, but messmen recruits trained directly under a senior messman who taught them how to address their officers, the posture they were to assume in the presence of officers, and the duties they were to perform. "Most in the class were high school graduates," Mouzon said, but the messmen were taught only "to serve—right side, left side, what to put here, what to put there."[18]

Mouzon also remembered Doris Miller as "a big gentle man." Tall and strong, he weighed between 225 and 235 pounds, and his feet were so large that he had to wear civilian shoes until the navy had a pair made for him. But despite his size, he was, "the nicest guy you ever want to meet."[19]

When on liberty in Norfolk, recruits had to wear leggings with their uniforms to distinguish them as "boots," that is, recruits in training. The black trainees hung out at the Titanic Bar on Church Street, and Mouzon said that "the first chance we'd get, we'd take off our leggings and relax—that is, all of us except for Doris. He went strictly by the book—even at the hang out."[20]

Upon completion of basic training, Miller received the grade of mess attendant, third class, and on 29 November 1939 was assigned to temporary duty aboard the ammunition ship USS *Pyro* (AE-1). While awaiting a permanent assignment, he served in the dining facilities, a duty he continued after 2 January 1940, when he was transferred to the battleship USS *West Virginia*.[21]

To a Waco newspaper's taunt that the navy offered blacks the opportunity of "totin' plates instead of cotton sacks," the city's black paper retorted that "the only way Negroes can die in Uncle Sam's democratic Navy is slinging hash." Regarding messmen's duties, assigned exclusively to men of color, Carlos Bulosan, a Filipino, commented, "I feel like a criminal running away from a crime I did not commit. And this crime is that I am a Filipino American."[22]

Twice that summer, from 14 through 22 June and from 1 July through 3 August 1940, Miller was assigned to temporary duty at the Secondary Battery Gunnery School aboard USS *Nevada*

(BB-36) to prepare him for his battle station, an antiaircraft battery magazine amidships. Fighting ships of the navy "required that every man aboard be trained and utilized at specific posts that are battle stations in the emergencies." Messmen were trained in shipboard drills at many jobs remote from their ratings and in battle were called upon to serve as handlers.[23] Aboard *Nevada*, Miller was taught to pass ammunition from the ship's magazine up to the gunners on the gun deck rather than having any part in the actual aiming or firing of the weapons.

Afterward, Miller returned to *West Virginia*, where, in common with almost every other black man in the navy, his primary duty was to serve food and bus tables in the junior officers' mess. He also volunteered as a room steward and made an extra five dollars each month doing laundry, shining shoes, and making beds for junior officers. He was also tasked with waking those going on duty. Particularly difficult to awaken was Ensign Edmond Jacoby. During the newly commissioned officer's first days aboard *West Virginia*, Miller would shake him awake. This was fine with Jacoby, but a senior officer reminded Miller that an enlisted man must never touch an officer. Thereafter, Miller would walk to within three inches of Jacoby's ear, shout "Hey, Jake!" and flee the room. But perhaps as an emotional outlet for his treatment as less than a man in the navy's warrior culture, the huge messman also entered the ship's boxing competitions and won its heavyweight division.[24]

With war increasingly likely, *West Virginia* was transferred to Pearl Harbor, Hawaii Territory, to guard against a potential Japanese attack. On 16 February 1941, just before *West Virginia* sailed for the Pacific, Miller received promotion to mess attendant second class. Moreover, the farm boy from McLennan County was granted his wish of traveling widely, making port in Cuba, Peru, Chile, Brazil, Uruguay, Argentina, and the Philippines. But when the ship docked in rigidly segregated Australian or New Zealand ports, black personnel were not allowed shore leave.

3

"God's Strength and Mother's Blessing"

The Attack on Pearl Harbor,
7 December 1941

෧ഝഎ

. . . And of course my blood was

Boiling about in my head and straining and howling and
   singing me on.

Of course I was rolled on wheels of my boy itch to get at the
   gun.

Of course all the delicate rehearsal shots of my childhood
   massed in mirage before me.

Of course I was child

And my first swallow of the liquor of battle bleeding black
   air dying and demon noise

Made me wild.

—Gwendolyn Brooks, "Negro Hero"[1]

On the morning of Sunday, 7 December 1941, Mess Attendant 2nd Class Doris Miller was awake at 6:00 a.m., collecting soiled laundry and looking forward to having the day off. Earlier that morning friends had invited him to join them on shore leave, but he had declined. His friend and fellow messman Hardwick Thompson had just returned from liberty following thirty days of confinement in the brig. Thompson had "stood a little too tall," as

he later put it, to an officer and had received the customary pun-
ishment for insubordination.[2]

That same Sunday morning, "a date," as Franklin D. Roosevelt
said, "which will live in infamy," Japan launched a surprise attack
on US military and naval bases on the Hawaiian island of Oahu.
At 7:48 the first wave of 353 dive bombers and torpedo bombers
hit the Pacific Naval Air Base, destroying or crippling thirty-six
seaplanes and killing or wounding eighty-four Americans. "All of
a sudden there was a noise overhead," Miller's friend and fellow
messman George Bland recalled sixty years later. "We began to re-
alize that these were not drills; they were the real McCoy."[3] Seven
minutes after the initial attack, the second wave hit Pearl Harbor,
where ninety-six unsuspecting US warships were riding at anchor.
The heart of the fleet—the battleships *West Virginia, Arizona, Tennessee, Maryland, Pennsylvania, Nevada,* and *Oklahoma*—were
moored along "Battleship Row," along Ford Island. *West Virginia*
was moored at berth F-6, outboard from the battleship *Tennessee,*
with forty feet of water beneath its keel.

The first of the nine Japanese Type 91 eighteen-inch aerial torpedoes to hit *West Virginia*'s port side was launched at 7:57 by Lt.
Cmdr. Shigeharu Murata of the Japanese aircraft carrier *Akagi.*
One hit the steering gear, dislodging the rudder, and at least three
struck below the armor belt, with one or more striking the belt
itself. One or two torpedoes exploded on the armored second deck
after entering the ship through holes made by previous torpedoes.

West Virginia was also struck by three Type 99 No. 80 Mk 5
bombs made from sixteen-inch armor-piercing naval shells fitted
with aerial fins. The first hit the foretop and penetrated the su-
perstructure deck, but failed to explode. The second hit farther
aft, destroying a Vought OS2U Kingfisher floatplane on the upper
catapult of turret three. The impact knocked a second floatplane
upside down to the main deck below, spilling gasoline from its
fuel tanks, which quickly ignited. The third bomb, also a dud, penetrated the four-inch turret roof, destroying one of the turret's two

guns as burning fuel from the overturned aircraft injured turret personnel and damaged the remaining gun.

Torpedo damage caused rapid compartment flooding, but counterflooding by damage-control parties under Lt. Comdr. John S. Harper, *West Virginia*'s first lieutenant and the third ranking officer aboard, and the closure of all water-tight hatches prevented the ship from capsizing. Even so, the ship was soon engulfed in an oil-fed conflagration, begun by the burning *Arizona* and sustained with fuel leaking from both ships.

In the meantime, the ship's captain, Mervin Sharp Bennion, had sustained a gaping wound in his abdomen, apparently caused by a fragment flying from the bridge of the stricken *Tennessee*. Ens. Victor Delano, a recent graduate of the US Naval Academy, found him "propped up against the side of the bridge and he was completely cut open, and he was holding his guts in." The ship's executive officer, Roscoe H. Hillenkoetter—later to become the first director of the Central Intelligence Agency—abandoned ship by jumping off the starboard quarterdeck. Notified by an officer on the conning tower that Captain Bennion was dying, Harper became the senior surviving officer.[4]

When the alarm for general quarters sounded that morning, Messman Miller dashed to his combat station, the antiaircraft battery magazine amidships, only to find "that torpedo damage had already rendered it untenable." He then resorted to "Times Square," the ship's central location where port-to-starboard and fore-to-aft passageways crossed, and reported himself available for other duty. In an interview with the *Pittsburgh Courier* in December 1942, Miller stated that "several men lost their lives—including some of the high officers—when the order came for volunteers from below to come on the upper deck and help fight the Japanese."[5]

Lt. Comdr. T. T. Beattie, *West Virginia*'s navigator, ordered Lt. Comdr. Doir C. Johnson, the ship's communications officer, to the bridge to bring the stricken captain down to the main deck. On his way to the bridge, Commander Johnson spotted "a very powerfully built individual" and, "having in mind that he might pick up the Captain and carry him below," ordered Miller to accompany him to the bridge. A runner also got word to Lt. Claude V. Ricketts, the ship's gunnery officer, who quickly reported to the bridge to help move the captain. En route to the bridge, the men felt a tremendous jolt, which Miller thought must have come from their own ship but later found was actually from an explosion aboard the nearby *Arizona*.[6]

Captain Bennion, lying on a cot in the starboard doorway to the admiral's walk, was still alert and issuing orders. Although he was rendered first aid by a pharmacist mate, no morphine was available to ease his pain because, Ensign Delano later wrote, "we were at peace and you don't put things like morphine" in a ship's first aid kit. Although the captain refused to leave his post, Lt. Cmdr. John Harper ordered Miller, along with Lieutenant Ricketts and Lt. (j.g.) Frederic H. White, to carry Bennion down from his exposed position on the damaged and blazing bridge to a place of greater safety on the ship's forecastle. Flames and smoke from an oil fire in the galley, the ship's list, and the bridge's constrictive layout conspired to foil every effort to lower the captain to the main deck without aggravating his horrific injury. So, "unable to lower their captain on an improvised stretcher" that sagged and almost broke, they moved him to a sheltered spot just aft of the conning tower, located below the navigation bridge and under the port side antiaircraft guns.[7]

While Lieutenant Ricketts gathered material to construct a stretcher on which to lower the captain to the main deck, Lieutenant White observed a pair of unmanned .50-caliber Browning antiaircraft machine guns and directed Miller to assist him in serving them. The port side antiaircraft guns had been silenced by the ship's list. The deck, tilted at a crazy angle, was awash with oil and water, and fires raged nearby, but most of the starboard guns were operational, so White ordered Miller to load while he and Ensign

Delano fired.[8] Miller had served both men as a room steward and knew them well. Delano, who expected Miller only to load both guns, was shocked to see him actually firing at dive-bombing Japanese planes.[9] "D. Miller, mess attendant second class, and I manned #1 and #2 machine guns forward of the conning tower," White later reported.[10]

Despite his lack of training, Miller drew on his early experience of squirrel hunting on the family farm, and by his own account, firing the machine gun came naturally. As he later recounted, "It wasn't hard. I just pulled the trigger and she worked fine. I had watched the others with these guns. I guess I fired her for about fifteen minutes. I think I got one of those Japanese planes. They were diving pretty close to us."[11]

Considerable controversy persists as to Miller's effectiveness. White reported that, having no training in the weapon, the messman's shooting was largely ineffective. In 1990 White, then retired as a naval captain, was interviewed for an article about Miller. He "didn't know very much about the machine gun, but I told him what to do and he went ahead and did it. He had a good eye."[12]

According to Lieutenant Commander Johnson, Miller was handling his gun well, "blazing away as though he had fired one all his life." Miller himself stated that "when the Japanese bombers attacked my ship at Pearl Harbor I forgot all about the fact that I and other Negro[e]s can be only messmen in the Navy and are not taught how to man an antiaircraft gun."[13] When a Waco journalist asked him, in December 1942, what he thought about when taking control of the gun, he answered, "They just looked like a lot of airplane. And there wasn't much to think about except shooting them. . . . I just thought I'd better hit those planes before they hit me."[14]

Later versions of the story had Miller shooting down as many as half a dozen Japanese planes. In an interview one year after the fact, Miller stated that he "ran up only to find that the officers who issued the order had been injured, so another fellow and I started to fire the big guns. And I actually downed four Japanese bombers. I might have brought down more—but I am positive of four."[15]

Although news stories have credited Miller with downing from two to five airplanes, these accounts have never been verified and are almost certainly apocryphal. During the time he was firing, only one Japanese plane was shot down. White reported that he saw Miller shooting, "but I would term it rather wild, so I doubt that he hit anything. I certainly did not see him shoot down a plane." Victor Delano related in 1993 one of the planes that Miller was shooting at went down. "He felt very pleased with that. And I don't blame him. But there were a lot of other guys shooting at it also." In fact, he said, "everyone else in the bay" was trying to bring it down.[16]

Walter Lord, in his bestselling account of Pearl Harbor, *Day of Infamy*, states that according to an unnamed witness, Miller was "a bigger menace than the Japanese." And according to Pearl Harbor historian David Aiken, the only plane within range of *West Virginia*'s guns to actually fall during the time the messman was "happily blazing away" was one of several D3A Bakugekiki ("Val") dive bombers that attacked *Maryland* from an approach over its port quarter, that is, from directly over *West Virginia*. Forensic evidence indicates its damage was primarily inflicted by a 1.1-inch gun from a battery aboard *Maryland*.[17]

A total of thirteen "Vals" had targeted *Maryland*. Seaman 1st Class Chris Beal was the "trainer" on *Maryland*'s 5-inch AA gun #4. "I saw a group of five come in from the port-quarter angle and a few bombs fell between *Maryland* and *Oklahoma* and we got mist of oily water on us," he recalled. "I still remember their 'banshee death wail' as they dived on us, then the whistle of bombs, near misses, and the engine re-gaining altitude as they pulled up over us."[18]

The planes were too fast for *Maryland*'s 5-inch guns, but not for the ship's 1.1-inch guns. Planes were coming on a straight course, which gave its gunners an almost-still target with an ever-decreasing range. Antiaircraft fire from the forward 1.1-inch gun on *Maryland*'s port side hit the second plane in the dive. Seaman Beal saw the damaged plane as it "smoked and made a rattling, irregular engine noise" and crashed east of Pearl Harbor. *Maryland*'s victory was officially claimed by the navy, and Japanese *kodochosho* (after-action reports) reveal this was the sole plane shot down near *West Virginia*.[19]

Miller, at first, told navy officials he thought he hit one of the planes. A naval officer on active duty—the author of *Battle Report*—asserted that "in the interest of a legend already in existence, it would be pleasant to be able to report that Miller shot down one or more planes. A careful [investigation] fails to bring forth either a contradiction or a substantiation in fact."[20] Although one quarter of the 353 attacking Japanese aircraft were reportedly hit by American fire, only 29 failed to return to their carriers. *West Virginia* received no official credit for shooting down any of them.[21]

Out of ammunition and with the intense heat driving them from their guns, White and Miller returned to the conning tower. There they found the signal bridge completely engulfed in flames and the navigation bridge burning to the starboard. By then Lieutenant Ricketts had located an eight-foot ladder, lashed Captain Bennion to it and tied a line to each end, and hoped to lower him to the boat deck. The attempt was unsuccessful due to the ship's list, and soon thereafter the boat deck was evacuated on account of a serious oil fire. Bennion insisted that he should remain behind, but Ricketts, White, Miller, and Chief Signalman A. A. Siewart passed a fire hose from *Tennessee* and continued to fight the flames until a pharmacist mate pronounced Captain Bennion dead.

Finding other means of escape blocked by flames, Miller, Ricketts, White, and one other man on the bridge escaped only when Ens. Henry F. Graham went up the starboard boat crane and sent over a line, which they secured to a rail on the bridge and then crossed to the crane, hand over hand, down to the boat deck.

After abandoning the bridge, White ordered Miller to help him pull sailors from the burning water onto the ship's deck, thus, as Commander Hillenkoetter reported, "unquestionably saving the lives of a number of people who might otherwise have been lost."[22] But by then, the ship was flooding below decks and rapidly settling in the harbor's shallow water. At about 2:00 p.m. *West Virginia*'s crew gave up the one-sided fight against the flames. With his ship sinking at its moorings, Lieutenant Commander Harper ordered the remaining crew members to abandon ship.[23]

Doris Miller was one of the last three men to leave *West Virginia*. He and his shipmates swam 300 or 400 yards to shore, avoiding patches of flaming oil from *Arizona*. Splashing ashore on Ford Island, Miller later told his brother Arthur James, "With those bullets spattering all around me, it was by the grace of God that I never got a scratch."[24] His niece, Vickie Miller, recorded that he told his mother that "it was God's protective hands" that had prevented him from being killed.[25]

He also told his cousin, Ernest Smith, that, in Smith's words, "when he got back to the dock and looked back at the ship, he had never been so afraid in all his life."[26] The young sailor spent that night on the beach where he talked for hours with fellow messman George Bland. "I guess we talked about what we saw," Bland later recalled. "It seemed like a dream that was not real. We were not anticipating that a war would start there."[27]

Of the 2,335 Americans killed that December morning, 1,102 were aboard the USS *Arizona*. Of *West Virginia*'s 1,541 crewmembers, 130 were killed and 52 wounded. Seven of the eight US battleships were sunk or badly damaged, and many cruisers and destroyers had been damaged as well. Six air bases were heavily damaged, and 188 US planes were destroyed on the ground and 150 more were damaged. The Japanese had lost only 55 men, three submarines, and 29 of their 353 attacking planes. Doris Miller attributed his survival to divine providence. "It must have been on God's strength and mother's blessing," he later told a reporter for the *Pittsburgh Courier*.[28]

4

"A Simple Act of Justice"

The Navy Cross

໑ແໆໆ໑

W hen she heard the news of the black sailor who had manned the machine gun during the Japanese attack, Henrietta Miller said, "That's got to be Doris they talking 'bout."[1] The US Navy, however, was a full year in determining and disclosing the identity of the heroic messman.

Within days of the disaster at Pearl Harbor, all of the surviving officers submitted after-action reports. These hundreds of reports were gathered by Lt. Cmdr. Paul C. Crosley, aide and flag secretary to the commander in chief of the Pacific Fleet, Adm. Husband Kimmel, and to his replacement, Adm. Chester W. Nimitz, who carried out the awarding of commendations to all personnel cited for outstanding performance. All of the officers aboard *West Virginia* mentioned the presence of the big mess attendant who, after discovering that his designated battle station had been destroyed, was ordered to the bridge to help carry Captain Bennion to safety.

Two weeks after the attack on Pearl Harbor, and following Secretary Franklin Knox's return from a fact-finding trip to Hawaii, government public relations officials released a number of stories of heroism "equal to any in U.S. naval history." Those reports referenced the actions of an unknown Negro sailor. Soon hearsay stories of Miller's actions on the day of the Pearl Harbor attack began to circulate. Some exaggerated versions had him downing several Japanese aircraft, and on 22 December 1941 the *New York Times* printed the sketchy testimony of an unidentified naval officer who supposedly served on *Arizona* describing a black sailor "who stood on the hot decks of his battleship and directed the fighting." This mess attendant, "who never before had fired a gun," the story went, "manned a machine gun on the bridge until his ammunition was exhausted."[2] The unknown messman was named to the 1941 Honor Roll of Race Relations. On New Year's Day, 1942, the navy released its list of commendations for heroism at Pearl Harbor. On the list was a single commendation for the as yet unnamed black sailor, and the Navy Board of Awards, established on 12 February 1942, recommended that he be considered for an award.[3]

On behalf of the NAACP, Emmett J. Scott, a special assistant to the secretary of war during World War I and a prominent black educator, wrote to Roosevelt and Knox presenting the case for Miller to be awarded the Distinguished Service Medal for an act of "raw courage." If Miller's deeds were not "of transcendent importance" in the defense of Pearl Harbor, he argued, they were "at least of vital importance to the cause of unified morale in our country."[4]

In February the Navy Department announced that "a colored messman . . . and two Negro workmen, along with four white men who labored heroically under fire during the vicious Japanese attack . . . may receive Naval awards."[5] On 12 March 1942, the same day that the Navy Board of Awards was established, Dr. Lawrence D. Reddick, a well-respected black historian at Temple University, informed the editor of the *Pittsburgh Courier*, after corresponding with the navy, that the "colored messman" was Doris Miller. Although the navy seemed loath to honor a black sailor as a hero, the African American community quickly accepted Miller as a symbol of black America's fighting pride and immediately recognized him as one of the "first US heroes of World War II."[6] On 14 March 1942, the *Pittsburgh Courier,* an influential voice among African

Americans and with over 250,000 weekly subscribers, released a story that named the black messman as "Dorie" Miller,[7] and on 21 March the paper initiated a write-in campaign to send Miller to the Naval Academy.[8] "To President Franklin D. Roosevelt," the newspaper's clip-out coupons read, "as commander in chief of the army and navy of the United States, as a token of national appreciation, colored America urges you to send Dorie Miller, messman hero of Pearl Harbor, to the Naval Academy for training."

Moreover, on the day following the announcement of his identity, although no one yet knew what deeds Miller had performed as the basis for such an award, Senator James Michael Mead, a New York Democrat, introduced a bill—Senate Resolution 2392—to award Miller the Congressional Medal of Honor. According to Mead, "the 12,000,000 loyal and patriotic Negro people will be cheered by this recognition of one of their own by the Congress—the United States House of Representatives and the Senate." Mead maintained that the bill was "a simple act of justice by those who represent a grateful nation."[9]

Four days later, Representative John D. Dingell Sr., a Michigan Democrat, introduced a matching bill—House Resolution 6800—calling upon the president to "present in the name of Congress a medal of honor to Dorie Miller, a second class mess attendant, in recognition of distinguished and courageous service at the risk of his life and above and beyond the call of duty while aboard a United States battleship at Pearl Harbor on December 7, 1941." Dingell was "convinced that Dorie Miller deserves to be honored with the Congressional Medal of Honor, and I intend to do everything in my power to see that he gets it."[10]

Although Mead and Dingell were seconded by the Fraternal Council of Churches, the Southern Negro Youth Council, and the National Negro Congress,[11] on 9 April 1942, Secretary of the Navy William Franklin (Frank) Knox sent a letter to Georgia Democrat Carl Vinson, the House of Representatives' chairman of naval affairs, that outlined the requirements of the Medal of Honor and stated that Miller's deeds were not deserving of the nation's highest award for valor. This infuriated African American activists. Awarding Miller the Medal of Honor would of course be criticized by those who would contend the messman did nothing more than what he was expected to do, indeed what he was ordered to do. Years later Juliete Parker, author of *A Man Named Doris,* maintained that the award was in fact scuttled by lawmakers from Miller's home state because of its notorious racist history.

Fifteen other young Americans won the nation's highest military commendation for heroism on that 7 December, and numerous historians and political leaders have pointed out that, gallant as their sacrifices were, Doris Miller's exploits aboard *West Virginia* were at least of equal distinction, and all the more deserving to be honored because of the oppressive racial stigma under which he performed so heroically. According to his Medal of Honor citation, R. Adm. Isaac Campbell Kidd, the commander of Battleship Division One at Pearl Harbor, "discharged his duties as Senior Officer Present Afloat until the U.S.S. *Arizona,* his Flagship, blew up from magazine explosions and a direct bomb hit on the bridge which resulted in the loss of his life." Capt. Franklin Van Valkenburgh, the commander of *Arizona,* "gallantly fought his ship" until it was destroyed by magazine explosions and a direct bomb hit on the bridge, "which resulted in the loss of his life." Lt. Cmdr. Samuel Glenn Fuqua directed the fighting of the fire and rescue of the wounded aboard *Arizona* in a manner that "resulted in the saving of many lives." As the senior surviving officer, he ordered that the ship be abandoned but maintained his position on the quarterdeck until all of the crew had been rescued. Lt. Cmdr. Donald Kirby Ross operated the forward dynamo room of *Nevada* until, blinded and rendered unconscious by smoke, steam, and heat, he was ordered to abandon his duty station. Cmdr. Cassin Young took personal command of USS *Vestal'*s three-inch antiaircraft gun until blown from the deck by the explosion of the forward magazine. Swimming back to the burning and sinking ship, he found himself to be the senior officer on board, where-upon he countermanded a junior officer's order to abandon ship and, "determining that such action was required to save his ship," with the assistance of a tugboat, ran *Vestal* aground. Lt. John Will Finn, stationed at the Kaneohe Bay Naval Air Station, received several wounds while manning a .50-caliber machine gun. Only when peremptorily ordered to seek medical attention did he abandon his post, but then returned to supervise the rearming of returning aircraft. Ens. Herbert Charpiot was mortally wounded by a bomb explosion aboard *California*. He refused to be evacuated, "saying, in words to the effect, 'Leave me alone! I am done for. Get out of here before the magazines go off.'" Ens. Francis C. Flaherty, aboard *Oklahoma*, "remained in a turret, holding a flashlight so the remainder of the turret crew could see to escape, thereby sacrificing his own life." Edwin Joseph Hill, chief boatswain of *Nevada*, "was blown overboard and killed" while attempting to let go of the ship's anchors. Gunner Jackson Charles Pharris, although severely injured by the initial Japanese bombing raid, set up a hand-supply ammunition train for the antiaircraft guns on *California* until the ship began to list heavily to port. He then dragged many of his unconscious shipmates to safety, saving many from death, and "was largely responsible for keeping *California* in action during the attack." Chief water tender Peter Tomich "remained at his post in the engineering plant of the U.S.S. *Utah* until he saw that all boilers were secured and all fireroom personnel had left their stations, and by so doing lost his life." Machinist's Mate 1st Class Robert Raymond Scott refused to leave his battle station aboard *California*, saying, "This is my station and I will stay . . . as long as the guns are going." He died in the flooded air compressor compartment. Chief radioman Thomas James Reeves, in a burning passageway, supplied ammunition to antiaircraft guns aboard *California* until, "overcome by smoke and fire," he died in action. Like his shipmate Ensign Flaherty, Seaman 1st Class James Richard Ward assisted the other members of his turret crew to escape at the cost of his own life. And Capt. Mervyn Sharp Bennion, Miller's commanding officer aboard *West Virginia*, was cited for "his apparent concern only in fighting and saving his ship," and, although mortally wounded, he "strongly protested against being carried from the bridge."[12]

Of those fifteen heroes, nine received their awards posthumously, having been killed in action that day, and most of the rest sustained severe wounds. Nine were officers, some quite senior, they were always at the head of the line when medals are bestowed. But none, either at Pearl Harbor or on any other battlefield of World War II, was black.

Leroy Ramsey, a veteran of World War II in the Pacific, a history professor from Albany, New York, the editor of *Black American Veteran*, and the author of *Black Americans in Defense of Our Country*, has been laboring since 1984 to have the Medal of Honor bestowed on Miller. According to Ramsey, "Because Miller was black, this is what makes his heroism so outstanding. The first thing that the Congressional Medal of Honor asks is, you have to go beyond the call of duty. That phrase cannot be lost when it comes to Dorie Miller. Here is a man who did what he was not allowed to do. Just manning that machine gun was going beyond the call of duty right there."[13]

Further, Captain Bennion, who was incapacitated throughout the action, received the Medal of Honor posthumously. Indeed, every flag or commanding officer who died at Pearl Harbor received the Medal of Honor for doing essentially what he was expected to do or, in most cases it seems, for being unable to do very much at all.

Senator Mead, however, was determined to push his bill through Congress, with or without Secretary Knox's approval. "I was elated as the pioneer in the movement to honor Doris Miller, the courageous mess attendant, who is one of the outstanding heroes of the Pearl Harbor attack," Mead told reporters.[14]

The raid on Pearl Harbor outraged Americans of all classes and colors. Initially blacks—calling for brotherhood and unity across racial lines—rallied with their white neighbors in defense efforts. But white racial prejudice persisted. As Charles Houston noted, the navy had warned for decades that racial integration would destroy its "battle efficiency," but Pearl Harbor had proved that "pure white battle efficiency" was a fallacy of monumental proportions, and that the present emergency demanded that the navy enlist and promote the best people available for each rating, regardless of race. Walter White, the NAACP's executive secretary, could not help but remind the nation in December 1941 that "at least blacks could not be made scapegoats for the country's naval fiasco. The naval department had seen to it that no blacks hold positions of responsibility—anywhere."[15]

The black press and such protest organizations as the NAACP campaigned relentlessly for full African American participation in the armed forces during World War II. They believed, as they had during World War I, that military service would convince whites to grant civil and social equality to African Americans. "Our country is at war," wrote W. E. B. Du Bois. "The war is critical, dangerous and world-wide. If this is our country, then this is our war." To Du Bois, the black American's first duty was clear: "We will not bargain with our loyalty."[16]

Despite such ugly incidents as the so-called "Fort Bragg Riot" of 12 August 1941 in which Pvt. Ned Truman was shot in the back after seizing the pistol of a military policeman who had struck him, declaring, "Goddam it! I'm goin' to break up you M.P.'s beating us colored soldiers," Walter White of the NAACP strongly believed that "blacks had to participate fully in the war effort if they were to press claims to full citizenship." Likewise, James G. Thompson firmly believed that, despite its flaws, the nation was worth defending. "Things will be different for the next generation," he wrote. "Colored Americans will come into their own, and America will become the true democracy it was designed to be. These things will become reality in time; but not through any relaxation of the efforts to secure them."[17] The Norfolk, Virginia, *Journal and Guide* wrote, "We are Americans—we are at war," maintaining that "so long as our service remains complete and unsullied, the cry for total emancipation is just inevitable."[18]

The largest and most influential part of the black leadership maintained its faith that the wholehearted support of the black community for the Allied war effort would ultimately win victory over American racism. Nevertheless, the spectacle of the United States fighting a worldwide crusade against German, Italian, and Japanese fascism when the US civilian and military social order was racially segregated and treated African Americans in a fascist manner created an enormous morale problem in the black community. As one federal official wrote in 1942, the lack of racial equality had given rise to "a sickly, negative attitude toward national goals."[19] America's racist treatment of black soldiers and sailors, its failure to end racial discrimination in defense employment, and its preservation of racial disenfranchisement and segregation in the South all instilled this apathy. One Cincinnati cleaning woman declared that it did not matter to her if Hitler won the war. "It couldn't be any worse for colored people—it may and it may not. It ain't so good now."[20]

More than any other cause, chronic racial violence and discrimination lowered black enthusiasm for the war. Journalist Earl Brown explained, "because he must fight discrimination to fight for his country and to earn a living, the Negro today is angry, resentful and utterly apathetic about the war."[21] Even those black men and women who supported the US war effort condemned the hypocrisy they found in American democracy. "But what of our wrongs, cry a million voices with strained faces and bitter eyes. Our wrongs are still wrong," Du Bois protested. "War does not excuse disenfranchisement, 'Jim Crow' cars and social injustices."[22] The country's racist treatment of black soldiers and sailors, its failure to end racial discrimination in defense employment, and its preservation of racial disenfranchisement and segregation in the South all contributed to a lukewarm attitude.

As one black soldier asked rhetorically, "Should I sacrifice to live 'half American'?"[23] Walter White observed that many black college students firmly believed that Hitler could not do more damage to the black community than American racial segregation, exclusion, and lynching.[24]

In May 1942 the *Pittsburgh Courier* ran a front-page article by Dr. Milton S.J. Wright, chairman of the Department of Economics and Political Science at Wilberforce University, one of the country's oldest and most respected predominately black institutions. Before the war, Wright had been granted an interview with Adolf Hitler. The Führer, Wright observed, maintained that American blacks "must be definitely a third class people" because they constantly allowed the whites to lynch, beat, and segregate them, without rising up against their oppressors. "Don't you think your people are destined perpetually to be slaves of one kind or another?" The question, apparently, was rhetorical. "Yes! Your people are a hopeless lot. I don't hate them. I pity the poor devils."[25]

In fact, poet Langston Hughes, in an essay called "Nazi and Dixie Nordics," wrote that if, as was claimed, the Germans were the victims of a mass psychosis, so were white Southerners. "As the Hitlerites treat the Jews, so they treat the Negro[e]s, in varying degree of viciousness ranging from the denial of educational opportunities to the denial of employment, and from buses that pass Negro[e]s by to jailers who beat and torture Negro prisoners, from the denial of the ballot to the denial of the right to live."[26]

The racial harmony promised by the united front evident in black and white communities in response to the fascist threat was severely threatened by race riots in Detroit, Harlem, and elsewhere during the war. In 1942, when blacks attempted to move into Detroit's Sojourner Truth housing project—which had been built for the black community—the white "improvement association" formed a picket line, burned crosses, and turned residents away. Federal intervention was required before black occupancy became possible. One year later—on 22 June 1943—the war's worst riot occurred when fights broke out between black and white men at Detroit's Belle Isle Park, the city's main recreational area. Civil disorder lasted for four days until again federal troops restored order on 24 June. Twenty-five African Americans and nine whites were dead and nearly 700 injured, with $2 million worth of property destroyed. The *Baltimore Afro-American* called the Detroit riot a warning that the black masses would resort to violence to bring about an end to racial oppression. Indeed, two months later, rioting erupted in Harlem, leaving six dead and $2 million worth of property damaged. Such tragedies caused many black Americans to doubt that their loyalty to the nation would be rewarded with full civil rights. Growing numbers of African Americans expressed only tepid support for the war effort, and some protested through draft dodging, desertion, or violence against white authority. In a poll taken in one southern city, 83 percent of 150 black college students said that blacks should not fight in the war, and at a conference early in 1942, 64 percent of black participants believed that the black community would not support the war.[27]

Many in the black community resented having to fight for the right to fight for a country that treated them so badly. Although, as the Federal Bureau of Investigation concluded, black Americans remained, to the highest degree, loyal to their country and willing to fight in its cause, disaffection with the war effort resulted in draft resisters who refused to fight "the white man's war."[28] The most notorious instance of black draft evasion came in 1942 when Elijah A. Muhammad, the head of the Nation of Islam, was arrested and charged with "inciting his followers to resist the draft." He was sentenced to five years in federal prison.[29]

Langston Hughes, however, reflected black support for the war in the lyrics to "Freedom Road," recorded by folk singer Josh White in 1942.

> Hand me my gun, let the bugle blow loud,
> I'm on my way with my head a-proud,

One objective I've got in view,
Is to keep a hold of freedom for me and you.

United we stand, divided we fall,
Let's make this land safe for one and all.
I've got a message, and you know it right,
Black and white together unite and fight.[30]

"Is it fair, honest or sensible," black newspaper columnist George Schuyler, writing in the *Pittsburgh Courier*, asked, "that this country, with its fate in the balance, should continue to bar Negro[e]s from service except in the mess department of the navy, when at the first sign of danger they so dramatically show their willingness to face death in defense of the Stars and Stripes?" The navy's racism, he pointed out, "must be comforting to Hitler, Mussolini, and the Japanese" since it reinforced their undemocratic ideas.[31]

Most blacks, therefore, determined to fight World War II on two fronts. One front was the war against the foreign enemy; the other front was a war against what Malcom X later called "the racist cancer that is malignant in the body of America" and in its armed forces. Jackie Robinson, a second lieutenant in the famed 761st "Black Panthers" Tank Battalion and, later, the first African American to play baseball in the major leagues, was court-martialed for refusing to sit in the back of a bus. Of his trial and acquittal he wrote, "It was a small victory, for I had learned that I was in two wars, one against the foreign enemy, the other against prejudice at home."[32]

In the midst of this racial turmoil on the domestic front, Doris Miller continued to fight the Japanese. With *West Virginia* sunk and not to be refloated for months, on 15 December 1941 Miller had been transferred to USS *Indianapolis* (CA-35), a Portland-class heavy cruiser, where he would serve for the next seventeen months. *Indianapolis* was assigned to Task Force 12, in consort with the heavy cruisers *Minneapolis*, *Pensacola*, and *San Francisco* as well as ten destroyers, and sent into Japanese-controlled waters in the South Pacific. "Mother, don't worry about me," Miller wrote, "and tell all my friends not to shed any tears for me, for when the dark clouds pass over, I'll be back on the sunny side."[33]

Indianapolis participated in the fleet's earliest foray into the Japanese-dominated Coral Sea. The ship's all-messman five-inch gun crew did well, but Miller was not a member. William Henry, the ship's "telephone talker," remembered Miller well. "I don't know about his formal training as a machine-gunner on the *West Virginia*, but I know with his background [as a youthful hunter] that he had to know something about weapons—probably since his youth in Texas. And it was natural for him to take over for the regular machine-gunner," recalled Henry. "I did hear him say that he had shot down *two* Japanese planes—not that he was bragging about it." His tour at the battery gunnery school in July 1940 might have qualified him to serve a gun, but his battle station remained in the "hole," handling ammunition.[34]

Task Force 12 saw its first action on 20 February 1942 about 350 miles south of Rabaul, New Britain, when it was attacked by two waves of Japanese bombers of nine planes each. A combat air patrol from the carrier *Lexington*, however, drove them away after a two-hour aerial fight. Again, on 10 May, the task force engaged the Japanese, with *Lexington*'s dive bombers and torpedo planes crossing the Owen Stanley mountain range to achieve a total surprise over the enemy bases at Lae and Salamaua.

In the meantime, stateside, the black press seized the story of Miller's Pearl Harbor exploits and pressured the navy to give him proper recognition. During the months that he was at sea, black leaders continued an unrelenting campaign for a suitable reward for their hero. Henrietta Miller was brought to New York City to receive a scroll "for distinguished service to America" on her son's behalf;[35] and early in March 1942, Congressman Vito Marcantonio of New York wrote a congratulatory letter to Mrs. Miller predicting the demise of the navy's Jim Crow policy:

> I have been informed that the courageous young man is your son, Dorie. Let me congratulate you. The entire nation is deeply proud of your son. His actions will be a source of inspiration to all young Americans as well as to the Negro people. He is a symbol of the determination of the Negro people to do everything possible to smash the Axis powers.
>
> The splendid action of your son in defense of our country brings us closer to the day when our navy will gladly accept the services of its Negro citizens in every capacity. Through you, let me wish Dorie Miller continued distinguished service in his country's cause.[36]

Most conspicuous among white proponents of racial integration was Congressman Wendell Willkie, Roosevelt's Republican opponent for the presidency in 1940. In his speeches before Congress and to constituents, Willkie frequently referred to Doris Miller and the unbending racism that limited him to the navy's messman branch. In April 1942, when asked how to go about changing the policy that kept black Americans from equality in the navy, he said, "It could be done immediately. No law would have to be passed. Just one thing is necessary. An order by the President or the Secretary of Navy would dispose of the Navy's color bar—just like that! . . . It's damned foolishness! That's all it is! . . . I think this country should make a pronouncement saying that all discrimination on account of race should end."[37]

In March 1942 Congressman Willkie spoke at the inaugural dinner of Freedom House—described as an independent watchdog organization dedicated to the international expansion of freedom and democracy—at New York's Commodore Hotel. Freedom House, the congressman proclaimed, symbolized freedom, and stated that its membership was dedicated to the advancement of freedom throughout the world. He paused to wonder, however, "whether we're not a little pharisaical or perhaps even presumptuous in our high-minded statements about freedom. Are we always as alert to practice it here at home as we are to proclaim it abroad? Do we accord freedom to all of our citizens?" Then referencing Doris Miller, he declared: "We have no further news of that boy and we know none of the details of his life except that single fine act of judgment and self-sacrificing courage. But there's one fact we know positively and exactly: he cannot enlist in the United States Navy and only for the reason that he was born with a black skin."[38]

A few weeks earlier, Willkie had attended a boxing match in Madison Square Garden where prizefighter Joe Louis, "a perfect specimen of physical manhood," defended his world championship in order to raise almost $100,000 for the Naval Relief Society. More recently he had heard Louis speak to 20,000 people at another Naval Relief Society rally in Madison Square Garden. It was, according to Willkie,

> a simple speech yet eloquent and moving. He was preparing to fight in an army uniform; he couldn't have been preparing to fight in a navy uniform for his skin was black. . . .
>
> Don't you think as American citizens, we should insist that our governments and Navy Department eliminate the bar that prohibits any American citizen from serving his country?[39]

A growing wave of editorials and letters charged the navy with delays and indifference to blacks in the armed forces. Even before the end of December 1941, Walter White had twice written to the Navy Department on Miller's behalf, pointing out that no citations for black personnel "had yet been received from the forces afloat for acts of gallantry or heroism during the attack" on Pearl Harbor and urging the president and the secretary of the navy "that the Distinguished Service Cross or other official recognition be given to this hero of the battle of Pearl Harbor. If the Negro mess attendant was killed in action, we urge that the medal be given posthumously. Without in any manner detracting from the heroism and gallantry under fire of white Americans who died at Pearl Harbor, we submit that the heroism of this Negro mess attendant merits special consideration in view of the fact that the policy of the United States navy in limiting Negro volunteers to service as mess attendants caused this and other Negro[e]s to go into situations of extreme danger in a far more vulnerable manner because they had been denied the opportunity to learn how to operate guns and other weapons of defense and offense."[40] Although White concluded by expressing his confidence that the secretary would make certain that "any acts of heroism will be fairly treated whether the men are black or white," his message was powerfully clear: black valor was being ignored.[41]

Such support for Miller, with its implied criticism of the navy—coming at a time when the service was attempting to recruit black sailors—forced Secretary Knox, on 30 December 1941, to direct his department to submit a report on Miller's eligibility for recognition to his office. On the next day, Knox responded personally to White's letter, stating that "an investigation will be made relative to the reported heroic action of the negro [sic] mess attendant" and promising that "the navy department will certainly recommend a proper recognition for any such heroic action."[42]

Three months passed, however, before any action occurred. Not until 5 March 1942 did the navy reply to White with a copy of Miller's service record.[43] Based upon the navy's revelations, on 13 March, Roy Wilkins of the NAACP called for Miller to receive the "highest official honor consistent with his performance at Pearl Harbor." In his letter to Secretary Knox, Wilkins stated the NAACP's ultimate goal. "Of course," he wrote, "the greatest honor that could be paid Mess Attendant Miller by the United States Navy would be for it to abolish forthwith the restrictions now in force . . . so that black Americans can serve their country and their navy in any capacity. This action by the navy would not only reward a hero, but would serve dramatic notice that this country is in fact a democracy in an all-out war against anti-democratic forces."[44]

On 21 March 1942 the *Pittsburgh Courier* demanded to know "why it required so long to identify Mr. Miller, and why to date he has received no reward for his heroism."[45] Forced by growing public opinion to recognize Miller's actions, on 1 April 1942, with apparent reluctance, Secretary Knox signed a letter of commendation citing Miller's "distinguished devotion to duty, extraordinary courage and disregard of his personal safety during the attack on the Fleet in Pearl Harbor on December 7, 1941." The terse letter merely stated that the black messman, "despite enemy strafing and bombing, and in the face of serious fire," had assisted in moving his stricken captain to a place of greater safety and had "later manned and operated a machine gun until ordered to leave the bridge."[46]

However, Secretary Knox continued to oppose pending legislation to award Miller the Medal of Honor, informing the House of Representatives Naval Affairs Committee on 9 April (as he did Edgar G. Browne, president of the National Negro Congress) that the letter of commendation, "in view of the recommendations of the Pacific Coast Fleet Board of Awards and CINCPAC [Commander in Chief of the Pacific Fleet], the recognition already awarded is deemed sufficient and appropriate." With no official support forthcoming, Mead's and Dingell's bills died in House and Senate committees.[47]

Further public pressure, however, quickly followed. On the day after Secretary Knox's commendation, CBS radio broadcast an episode of the series "They Live Forever," dramatizing Miller's deeds, and several African American organizations began a campaign to give Miller additional recognition. During the All-Southern Negro Youth Conference of 17–19 April, a signature campaign was launched, urging Congress to give Miller a suitable memorial, and his parents were brought to the conference and presented with a $100 defense bond.[48]

By March 1942, with Henrietta Miller's cooperation, color prints were being sold door-to-door in order to "see that every Negro home" could display a picture of the hero of Pearl Harbor. The print did not resemble Miller at all, but profits from its sale did enable the Miller family to move out of its tenant house and into a more substantial home in Waco. More important, Miller's growing popularity underscored the high regard that African Americans held for their hero.

In view of the massive interest shown by the African American community, on 1 May 1942 Attorney General Francis Beverley Biddle suggested in a letter to Roosevelt that "it would be a splendid thing to have the Navy decorate Miller." Knox's commendation, he pointed out, "is all the Navy wants to do," despite Miller's "distinguished devotion to duty, extraordinary courage and disregard for his own personal safety." Moreover, Biddle attached a stack of newspaper clippings, mostly from the *Pittsburgh Courier*, with such headlines as "U.S. Fails to Honor Hero Dorie Miller," "Messman Hero of Pearl Harbor Should Be Honored," and "Congress Hears Pleas for Honors for Doris Miller." Perceiving the political impact of such an act, as well as its moral imperative, Biddle quietly advised the president, "You may wish to urge the award of a medal." Roosevelt forwarded Biddle's letter to Knox with the rather pointed note, "Will you speak to me about this?"[49]

On 10 May the National Negro Congress—which, ironically, was one of the eleven organizations that Attorney General Biddle investigated as "subversive" and allegedly under the control of the Soviet Union—denounced Knox's recommendation denying Miller the Medal of Honor.

Under such intense pressure from the African American community, on 11 May 1942 President Roosevelt approved granting Miller the Navy Cross—at the time the third-highest US Navy award for gallantry during combat.

By then, black America wanted to welcome home its hero and pay him direct homage. A delegation from the NAACP, the National Negro Congress, and the *Pittsburgh Courier* sought the assistance of Addison Walker, special assistant to the secretary of navy, to bring Miller to Washington, DC, and to have the medal presented by President Roosevelt in person. On 13 May Walker advised Assistant Secretary of the Navy Ralph Bard that the NAACP's Washington, DC, chapter was planning a Doris Miller rally to be held on 31 May at the Lincoln Memorial. Such celebrities as Paul Robeson and Marian Anderson agreed to attend, and Walker requested that Miller be transferred to Washington to receive his award. Walker's memo to Bard ended with the observation that Miller was "probably replacing Joe Louis" as the greatest African American hero. Miller exhibited another "example of courageous fighting," he wrote, "which might well direct the emotions of 13,000,000 Negro[e]s into the right channel and contribute to general unity." But Doris Miller could not be delivered to Washington for the rally.[50]

The navy reported that Miller and his ship were engaged with the Japanese in the South Pacific.[51] So *Indianapolis,* then en route to the Aleutian Islands, made a brief stop in Hawaii where, on 27 May 1942, Miller was presented the Navy Cross by a fellow Texan, Adm. Chester W. Nimitz, the commander in chief of the Pacific Fleet, in a ceremony on the flight deck of the aircraft carrier *Enterprise* at Pearl Harbor, where much of the wreckage from the Japanese attack remained evident.[52] In 1940, as chief of the Naval Bureau, Admiral Nimitz had declared that "after many years of experience, the policy of not enlisting men of the Colored race for any branch of the naval service except the messmen's branch was adopted to meet the best interests of general ship efficiency." But now Nimitz stated that Miller's award "marks the first time in this conflict that such high tribute has been made in the Pacific Fleet to a member of his race and I'm sure that the future will see others similarly honored for brave acts."[53]

Connery and Henrietta Miller, 1942 (Thomas E. Turner Papers, Texas Collection, Baylor University)

DORIS MILLER
The Hero of Pearl Harbor, December 7, 1941

Mess Attendant 2nd Class Doris Miller (Thomas E. Turner
Papers, Texas Collection, Baylor University)

USS *West Virginia* (BB-48) (US Navy photograph, National Archives)

Battleship Row under Japanese attack, Pearl Harbor, Hawaii Territory, 7 December 1941 (Japanese reconnaissance photograph, Wikipedia)

Charles Henry Alston's "December 7th—Remember!!" depicting Miller
shooting down a Japanese plane (Office for Emergency Management, Office
of War Information, Domestic Operations Branch)

Cuba Gooding Jr. as Doris Miller in *Pearl Harbor* (Touchstone Pictures, 2001)

USS *West Virginia*, damaged by Japanese bombs and torpedoes, afire and listing (US Navy, Library of Congress Prints and Photographs Division, Washington, DC)

Admiral Chester W. Nimitz reading citation to Doris Miller's Navy Cross, USS *Enterprise*, Pearl Harbor, 27 May 1942

Admiral Nimitz presenting Miller's Navy Cross (Library of Congress Prints and Photographs Division, Washington, DC)

Doris Miller addressing graduating class from Camp Robert Smalls, Great Lakes Naval Training Station, 13 January 1943 (US Navy photograph, National Archives)

Doris Miller talking with sailors and a civilian, Great Lakes, 13 January 1943 (Naval History and Heritage Command)

Lt. Cmdr. Daniel W. Armstrong [in khaki uniform] presenting George Clinton Fields, former valet to President Franklin D. Roosevelt, with certificate of graduation from Camp Robert Smalls, Naval Training Station, 13 January 1943 (US Navy photograph, National Archives)

George Clinton Fields with certificate of graduation from Camp Robert Smalls, Great Lakes Naval Training Station, 13 January 1943 (US Navy photograph, National Archives)

Doris Miller with friend on last leave

New Year's Eve, 1942

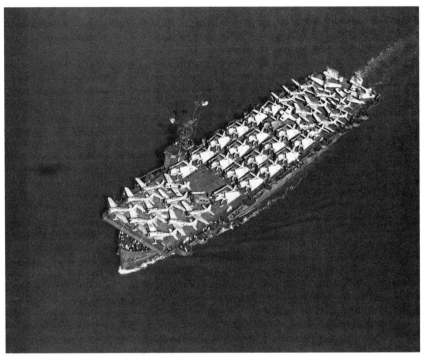

Escort Carrier USS *Liscome Bay* (CVE-56), "Combustible, Vulnerable, Expendable"
(US Navy photograph, National Archives)

"Above and Beyond the Call of Duty," US Navy recruiting poster featuring Miller designed by David Stone Martin, 1943 (Library of Congress Prints and Photographs Division, Washington, DC)

High School, May 5, 1944, dedication of the Doris Miller Memorial. Photo courtesy Baylor Texas Collection

Dedication of Doris Miller Monument, A. J. Moore High School (Thomas E. Turner Papers, Texas Collection, Baylor University)

Flag-draped Doris Miller Monument (Thomas E. Turner Papers, Texas Collection, Baylor University)

Postage stamp honoring Doris Miller, issued on
4 February 2010 in the Distinguished Sailors series
(US Postal Service)

Congresswoman Barbara Jordan speaking at the commissioning of USS
Doris Miller (DE-1091) 30 June 1973 (Courtesy Captain Lynn P. Blasch's
Photos)

5

"An Everlasting Inspiration"

Jim Crow in Retreat

ᏅᎢᎢᎢᎥᎧ

The African American community responded to Miller's re-
nown with renewed loyalty to their homeland and with a
determination to seize this new opportunity to better their lot
within it. At the same time, however, the *Dallas Express* pointed
out that none of the nation's 13 million black men could "serve in
the navy except as menials."[1] And indeed, two weeks after Pearl
Harbor, the navy announced that "the enlistment of Negroes
other than as mess attendants leads to destructive and undermining conditions." A special committee created by Secretary
Knox in July 1941 found there to be no discrimination because
the characteristics of blacks made them fit solely for messman's
duties. "The Navy insists even more strongly that it cannot take
a chance on a social experiment," the Knox committee stated.
"Since racial integration on naval units implies much more than
any other service, the Navy feels that it cannot [be] justly expected to be so far ahead of the nation's general habits in racial
matters as the advocates of full integration."[2]

Even before the outbreak of the war, on 27 September 1940,
Walter White, then executive secretary of the NAACP; T. Arnold
Hill of the National Urban League; and Asa Phillip Randolph,
president of the Brotherhood of Sleeping Car Porters, had brought

to Roosevelt a list of seven demands. They insisted that black officers and men be assigned on the basis of merit, not race; that more black officers be trained; that African Americans be allowed to serve in the air corps; that blacks be allowed to participate in the selective service process; that black women be permitted to serve as nurses; and that "existing units of the army and units to be established should be required to accept and select officers and enlisted personnel without regard to race." Although Roosevelt initially seemed receptive to these ideas, he later signed policy statements reaffirming segregation in the military and establishing racial quotas to limit black participation to 9 percent.[3]

During the course of World War II, the navy's policy toward black sailors evolved through three stages. A full year before the attack on Pearl Harbor, the Defense Committee of Franklin Roosevelt's Conference on the Participation of the Negro in National Defense, held at the Hampton Institute in November 1940, had condemned the navy, which still accepted black recruits as messmen only, as "the most undemocratic and un-American aspect of our Government."[4]

In response, on 2 July 1941, Secretary Knox created a committee, consisting of two naval officers, one Marine Corps officer, and a special assistant to the secretary, "for the purpose of investigating and reporting . . . the extent to which the enlisted personnel of the Navy and Marine Corps is representative of all United States Citizens, and in case there should be any evidence of discrimination because of race, creed, color or national origin, to suggest corrections." The committee, "by oral instructions," limited its inquiry "to the existing relationship between the United States Navy, United States Marine Corps and the Negro race."[5]

After holding three meetings, the committee reported that few of the blacks recruited into the navy prior to 1922 "qualified for advancement except for ratings where little or no military command must be exercised." The committee's staggeringly racist final report, completed on 21 December 1941 but never released to the public, concluded that "the enlistment of Negroes (other than as mess attendants) leads to disruptive and undermining conditions" and that "within the limitations of the characteristics and intelligence of members of certain races, the enlisted personnel of the Naval Establishment is representative of all the citizens of the United States. Therefore, no corrective measures are necessary."[6]

Of the 300 black men who volunteered for naval service in New York City alone in the days immediately following the attack on Pearl Harbor, none were accepted except as menials. With the navy's pressing need for additional manpower, however, during the second stage blacks were accepted for general service, but they still served under segregated conditions, in both training and assignment.

Although Secretary Knox had reportedly told President Roosevelt that if he were forced to integrate the navy, he would resign, under the increasing demand for additional personnel to man the fleets and the growing pressure to provide more equal opportunities for black recruits, on 7 April 1942 Knox announced that the navy would begin to accept black inductees into general service. Effective 1 June the navy began to accept black volunteers for training as radiomen, boatswain's mates, radar operators, gunner's mates, and other ratings besides the messman's branch. Under Knox's new dispensation, black volunteers were to receive basic and advanced training in segregated units, and after graduation from service schools they would be assigned to their specialties. Even as late as 1944 and 1945, however, nearly one-third of the incoming black recruits at the Great Lakes Naval Training Station were below the minimum education standard for the navy and were thus deemed ineligible for any specialized training. Those who did complete basic training at Great Lakes were neither permitted to serve in their specialties nor assigned to seagoing vessels, but were assigned ashore, principally to construction battalions, supply depots, ordnance stations, and harbor craft and were commanded by white officers and petty officers, at least until African American petty officers could be trained. No black officers would be commissioned. Knox termed the new program "an experiment."[7]

Some African Americans saw Knox's change in policy as a step, however small, in the right direction. The NAACP viewed it as "progress toward a more enlightened point of view," and John P. Davis, executive secretary of the National Negro Congress, congratulated Knox, calling his reforms a "bold, patriotic action in smashing age-old color restrictions which had prevented Negro people from full service in the United States Navy." Now, wrote Davis, "the heroic tradition of Dorie Miller at Pearl Harbor will serve as an everlasting inspiration" to every young man "to more fully serve his country and the navy."[8]

The *Pittsburgh Courier* acknowledged that Knox's "cracking of that door" was a step in the right direction, but insisted that the new policy fell short of appropriate reform. Viewing Knox's new policy even more favorably, the *Houston Informer* asked its readers who was offended by the navy's new stance on the employment of black sailors except for the more radical element of the black leadership? "Does it expect them to commit treason and order Negro[e]s not to enter the Navy? This is a war, and Negro leaders will do their race a great disservice if they permit themselves to forget that fact at any stage of their fight for their rights."[9]

Others, however, viewed the policy change as merely the "delivery of an insult to all defenders of democracy" and attacked those who lauded it as "accommodationist." As an editorial in the *Philadelphia Tribune* protested, "Secretary Knox's statements explaining the new policy did more to injure the morale of colored people than if the ban against Negro[e]s had remained in full force and effect. If Secretary Knox feels that it is necessary to cater to the prejudices of Navy officials in order to win this war for 'Freedom,' then it would be wiser for him to keep quiet."[10]

As always, outspoken in the defense of equality for black people, the *Pittsburgh Courier* pointed to the self-evident fact that "white and black and yellow and brown heroes are all shedding the same red blood for freedom's cause. Black and yellow and brown people have the same pride in their heroes that white people have in theirs." Nevertheless, the Navy Department had given black Americans "little enough opportunity and little enough encouragement." The *Courier's* outraged editor pointed out that the navy

> has offered to Negroes a limited training program and asked
> them to be happy about it. It has suggested to Negroes that
> they try to make good under this limited segregated pro-
> gram. It has hinted that if they make good under this restric-
> tive program the Navy Department may, out of the goodness
> of its heart, open the doors a little wider.
>
> Such an attitude is insulting to citizens who believe in
> themselves and the nation they have helped to build. No such
> proposition would be put to any other class of American
> citizens. Negroes want no concessions from the navy. They
> want the same privileges and opportunities for service and
> sacrifice and advancement vouchsafed to all other citizens.

Blacks, the editorial read, wanted every branch of the naval service, including naval aviation, opened to them on the basis of merit. They demanded command positions within the fleet "if they show ability," and they deplored "artificial barriers or rules and regulations obstructing their advancement and service."[11]

A. Phillip Randolph, president of the Brotherhood of Sleeping Car Porters, complained that the change "accepts and extends and consolidates the policy of Jim Crowism in the navy" as well as proclaims "an accepted, recognized government ideology that the Negro is inferior to the white man." The black magazine *Opportunity*, in its May 1942 issue, criticized Secretary Knox and the navy's policy, stating that "they might have provided for the training of small units of white and Negro boys together as an experiment," and suggested that naval officer training classes ought to be conducted at "those universities and colleges which now admit Negro[e]s as students." Knox opted, however, "to perpetuate and extend second-class status for citizens of color. Faced

with a great opportunity to strengthen the forces of democracy,"
Opportunity objected, "the Navy Department chose to affirm the
charge that Japan is making against America to the brown people
of East Asia," that "the so-called 'Four Freedoms' are for white
men only."[12]

In consequence of the navy's continued segregation, black enlistments remained low. In 1943 only 26,000 blacks were in the US
Navy—2 percent of the total enlisted strength. Two-thirds of them
were still messmen, and the remainder were confined to shore
duty units, loading and unloading ammunition ships or doing
construction work. The navy's policy placed what the *Pittsburgh
Courier* called "undue and unhappy emphasis" on the requirement
for black sailors to work in construction crews in navy yards. "We
simply do not want too much of that. We do not mind doing our
share of the work. But we want to do our full share of the fighting,
too. We strongly protest any plans which the navy may be hatching
to herd Negro[e]s into construction crews," the *Courier* protested.
"That was salt in an old wound."[13]

Further, Knox affirmed that there were "no plans" to allow
blacks to rise above noncommissioned grades.[14] "Well, he may
have no plans," retorted the *Courier*, "but we intend to require him
to formulate some plans. It is just as arbitrary, unconstitutional
and illegal to restrict any class of Americans to non-commissioned
grades as it is to restrict any class to the messman branch." The
Navy Department announced that it wished to proceed in a spirit
of "cordial experimentation," but that was what the *Courier* considered "a left-handed way of saying it wants Negro[e]s to stop
cussing and co-operate. It is the navy's job and responsibility to
convince Negro[e]s that it sincerely desires to co-operate."[15]

Thomas L. Brown, president of New York's Interracial Club,
also condemned the "two-race" navy policy. "There is nothing
here that merits either hailing or gratification. Militancy and mass
resentment have caused the administration to make this gesture,
ineffective though it is. Militancy must be continued; the struggle

must be more firmly and courageously conducted until the scourge of Jim Crow is entirely wiped out."[16]

The NAACP, as well, was bitterly critical of Knox's comments, stating that "he has clearly demonstrated his lack of the necessary capacity to serve our country in this perilous period. This blow to the morale of the Negro people will be deeply appreciated in Berlin, Rome and Tokyo." James Scott, president of the Washington, DC, branch of the NAACP urged President Roosevelt to remove Knox from his post. The national office of the NAACP declared itself "glad that the navy's policy has been revised" but wondered "if the change is not more apparent than real?"[17]

On the home front, the black press continued to agitate against domestic racism through the constant exposure of racial discrimination in jobs, housing, and civil rights, and the NAACP and the National Urban League also endeavored to enlist their members in an effort that, they believed, would lead to an ending of racial discrimination. Fearful, however, that white America might perceive this campaign as subversive to the nation's fight against Germany and Japan, the editors were quick to protest that "no one must interpret this militancy of Negroes as a plot to impede the war effort. Negroes recognize that the first factor in the survival of this nation is the winning of the war. But they feel the integration of Negroes into the whole scheme of things 'revitalizes' the U.S. war program."[18]

In a 31 January 1942 letter to the editor of the *Pittsburgh Courier,* James G. Thompson urged that a campaign for victory at home and abroad would allay the confusion felt by black Americans. In response, as an expression of both its patriotism and its need to carry on the fight against racism at home, the *Courier,* under the brilliant leadership of its editor, Robert Vann, initiated a campaign calling for "victory at home and abroad for the non-white races of America." The *Courier* launched its "Double V" campaign on 7 February 1942, demanding that Americans of color risking their lives abroad for victory over the Axis be rewarded with a victory on the home front in the form of full citizenship rights for all blacks. In a 14 February editorial, the *Courier* stated, "This slogan represents the true battle cry of colored America." As the newspaper explained its new agenda, "Americans all, are involved in a gigantic war effort to assure victory for the cause of freedom—the four freedoms so nobly expressed by President Roosevelt and Prime Minister Churchill. We, as colored Americans, are determined to protect our country, our form of government and the freedoms which we cherish for ourselves and for the rest of the world." Other black newspapers picked up the offensive, and it became a national phenomenon.[19]

The "Double V" campaign urged America to not only preach democracy abroad but to practice it at home. As Americans of color, they were determined to protect their country, their democratic government, and the freedoms they cherished for themselves and for the rest of the world. In their fight for freedom and equality, therefore, they waged "a two-pronged attack against our enslavers at home and those abroad who would enslave us. WE HAVE A STAKE IN THIS FIGHT. . . . WE ARE AMERICANS TOO!"[20]

The newspapers carried intensive coverage of the exploits of black servicemen and at the same time exposed the ongoing racial abuse of those soldiers. Stories, such as those of Doris Miller, were a powerful inspiration to the civilian black community to support the war against fascism. Miller himself was a supporter of the "Double V," writing to the *Courier* from aboard the *Indianapolis*, "Your work and constant sacrifice has not been a failure, and we ourselves have contributed so little to that which we should have in order to make faster progress. I also believe our 'Double V' for victory is a staunch and sound foundation towards our goal for greater and better inspiration for our people."[21] Small but welcome improvements became evident in the lot of black soldiers and sailors as the armed forces slowly began to ease their segregationist policy.[22]

The roots of the "Double V" campaign went back to 1941. Prior to the United States' entry into World War II, 75 percent of black Americans resided in the South, 90 percent lived in poverty, and only 25 percent had a high school education. One-third of employed black men were sharecroppers or tenant farmers, many of whom were mired in hopeless debt. The defense industry created jobs that brought about social and legislative reform, but as injurious to the wartime African American community as racial exclusion and segregation in the armed forces was the exclusion from employment in the fast-growing defense industries. Those industries were helping to lift the country out of the Great Depression, and African Americans had to be included in that process. For many African Americans, the war offered an opportunity to escape the grinding rural poverty of growing cotton on another man's farm, but blacks were left behind as the economy geared up for war. Six months after the bombing of Pearl Harbor, slightly more than half—144,853—of the 282,245 war-related job openings were reserved for whites only. In Texas, African Americans were barred from more than 9,000 out of the 17,435 openings for defense jobs.[23]

Responding to the blatant discrimination on the part of industry and governments, Asa Phillip Randolph, Walter White, and Lester Granger of the Urban League launched the March on Washington movement, which pledged to mobilize 100,000 African Americans to march down Pennsylvania Avenue on 1 July 1941 demanding a fair share of jobs and an end to segregation in government departments and the armed forces. The movement asked President Roosevelt to issue an executive order banning such discrimination. Eleanor Roosevelt met with Randolph and White to convince them to call off the march, and the president himself held a meeting with Randolph and other march leaders, including Benjamin Franklin McLaurin, an organizer and vice president of the International Brotherhood of Sleeping Car

Porters, in June 1941. McClaurin later recalled that Roosevelt was charming and affable, but evasive. Randolph remained stubborn and determined, refusing to call off the march unless the president issued an executive order. Eventually, Roosevelt agreed to work out a compromise, signing Executive Order 8802, which banned employment discrimination in the defense industry and government. The order also created a temporary Fair Employment Practices Committee to help ensure that defense manufacturers would not practice racial discrimination. Randolph agreed to call off the march.[24]

In the third and final phase of the navy's reluctant movement toward equal treatment for its black sailors, under prodding from the Special Programs Unit and the demands of civil rights leaders, Secretary Knox agreed to an experiment that would place African American crews aboard two deepwater vessels, albeit with white officers and petty officers above them.[25] The navy also opened a modest officer training program at Camp Robert Smalls on the Great Lakes Naval Training Station, with the first class comprising sixteen men. The predicted rate of washout was 25 percent, but, to the amazement of those in charge, everyone passed. The Bureau of Personnel could not bring itself to award commissions to all and arbitrarily made ensigns of twelve, with the thirteenth candidate rated as a warrant officer. The three not chosen remained enlisted men. Although the newly commissioned black sailors were not welcomed at the officers' club, they referred to themselves as "the Golden Thirteen."[26]

Navy secretary Franklin Knox died on 28 April 1944 and was replaced by James V. Forrestal, a liberal New York attorney and member of the Urban League. Thereafter, progress for blacks in the navy came more speedily. In July 1944 Forrestal announced that separate facilities and quotas were impractical; in June of the following year Camp Robert Smalls was closed, and separate training camps and programs were abolished.

Ironically, Doris Miller himself chose to remain a messman rather than becoming a gunner, machinist, radioman, or engineer. Rather, he saw the skills that he was learning in the galley as excellent training for going into business after the war.[27] His intention, once the war was over, was to marry his girlfriend, Mozelle Alexander of Flint, Texas, then a home economics major at Tillotson College in Austin, and, if he did not reenlist in the navy, to "go into the nightclub business somewhere on the coast. I think I'd like that."[28] In October 1943, however, Miller told a reporter for the *California Eagle* that he had been assigned to receive gunnery instruction in the near future and that perhaps he would become a prizefighter upon leaving the navy.[29]

6

"Tell All My Friends Not to Shed
Any Tears for Me"

To Tarawa and Beyond

⟳

Although the *Waco Times-Herald* all but ignored the hometown hero, mentioning Doris Miller in only a single para-
graph three weeks after he received the Navy Cross, black America
was jubilant, and elevated Miller above even the great Joe Louis as
its "number one hero." In June 1942 the *Pittsburgh Courier* called
for Miller to be returned to the States for a war bond tour, just
as several white heroes had been. "Why can't Dorie Miller, the
messman who risked his life to save that of his dying captain at
Pearl Harbor, be returned to his country so people may see him?
Why does the navy department find it so easy to return other
men—commanders of battleships, commanders of submarines and
destroyers, aviators and other personnel—and so difficult to return the heroic mess boy, Dorie Miller?" A later editorial featured
Miller's photograph with the caption "He Fought . . . Keeps Mop,"
while a white hero of the Pearl Harbor attack received an officer's
commission. The implication, the *Courier* sardonically suggested,
was that Miller was "too important waiting tables in the Pacific to
return him."[1]

If Secretary Knox were to demonstrate "forthrightness," the
Courier maintained, barriers to black service "would vanish over-

night. A simple, a routine order from Secretary Knox would bring Doris Miller back to the United States." The paper demanded that Knox order him home "so that he may perform the same service among his people that the white heroes are performing among their people. If they are needed, he is needed. If they can be spared, he can be spared."[2]

In furtherance of its campaign, the *Courier* secured an early July meeting for Henrietta Miller with Wendell Willkie in his New York office. At Mrs. Miller's behest, Willkie wrote to Knox, requesting that Miller be returned to the United States. New York's popular mayor, Fiorello LaGuardia, also agreed to work toward Miller's return to the States. "I think it would be a good thing to bring Dorie Miller back," he said.[3]

Miller, himself, was eager to return home. As he wrote to the *Courier* on 26 September, "I do hope your paper will continue the campaign in my behalf. It would be a great pleasure to get back for only a few days."[4] The campaign bore fruit when, while still attached to the heavy cruiser *Indianapolis,* Miller was ordered on a war bond tour. After nearly a year at sea, including six months patrolling waters off the Aleutian Islands, Miller arrived at Pearl Harbor on 23 November 1942, having been promoted to mess attendant first class on 1 June 1942. "A hero returns," exclaimed the *Courier.* "A medal he wears."[5]

Over the course of the next month Miller gave talks in Oakland, California; in his hometown of Waco; and in Dallas, promoting war bond sales and accepting tokens of admiration from black communities.[6] In an interview with the *Pittsburgh Courier* in Oakland on 7 December, Miller was asked if he considered it "quite a coincidence" that he was back in the States, exactly a year after Pearl Harbor. "It is something, all right," Miller replied, "You see, I have done quite a bit of traveling and have seen plenty of action. During the past year, I've sailed to Australia, Samoa, Alaska, Panama, Cuba, and now California."[7]

In Oakland, as well, Miller attended a special service at the First

African Methodist Episcopal Church, which presented him with a gold Christian cross, after which he shook hands with the entire congregation and autographed more than 200 albums and programs.[8]

Miller then headed south, first to Montgomery, Alabama, where Marion Beach later recalled seeing him at a war bond rally when she was sixteen years old and where her mother bought her an $18.00 "Dorie Bond."

Childhood friend Oscar Reese, then a student at Tillotson College in Austin, remembered that when "Dorie" came home to Waco for Christmas leave "he was just a big giant over me. He wasn't a real loud person or anything. He was real intelligent, kind of quiet like."[9] He was wearing his Navy Cross as well as an "E" for gunnery excellence and a red stripe indicating three years of service sewn on the sleeve of his uniform, but the hero of Pearl Harbor talked little about his war experiences. This was because, his father told a reporter, "he said it made him think of his dead buddies."[10]

Congresswoman Eddie Bernice Johnson of Dallas, who had turned six in Waco just days before Pearl Harbor, remembered that Miller "lived on the edge of the neighborhood where I grew up." She recalled "a big party" when Miller came home. "I don't know if I was there or not but I did walk around with my father to collect money for an ID bracelet. It was silver." For Johnson, Miller remained forever the young black hometown hero. "To the black Americans at the time and every moment since, he was the one that prevented us from having war on these shores in the U.S.," she said.[11]

The Miller family was entertained at the downtown Raleigh Hotel—the first time that blacks had been admitted as guests in the hotel's ballroom—and at Waco's Elizabeth Lee Center, which was "festooned with appropriate patriotic decorations." Seven-year-old Barbara Brown of Atlantic City, New Jersey, was "thrilled beyond measure" to dance with her hero. "I will be able to tell the pupils in my class at home that I've actually met Mr. Miller." On the following Thursday night the Millers were again entertained at the Shadowland, a popular Waco nightspot, with a party that lasted from 10:00 p.m. until 1:00 a.m. The festivities, attended by "representatives from several of the women's clubs of the city" as well as soldiers from the Waco Army Flying School and others home on furlough, contributed to "the spirit of the holiday season."[12]

In Dallas on 28 December 1942, Miller was the guest of honor at a dinner at the Moorland Branch of the YMCA. He spoke briefly and was presented with a silver "armband" inscribed with his name. On 14 January Miller was the guest of honor at a dinner at the Moorland Branch of the YMCA, where he spoke briefly, and on 19 January he spoke to the New Hope Colored Baptist Church, where he was presented with a Bible bound in navy blue. Although according to the *Dallas Morning News*, he "modestly and politely declined to talk about his experiences" at Pearl Harbor, stating instead that he was anxious to return to active duty, Miller did say that "there wasn't time to think. It just seemed like the thing to do."[13]

The following day Miller addressed the 850 students of Dallas's Julia C. Frazier School, telling them that although he was not trained as a gunner, "when he saw his captain shot there was only one thing to do: Shoot the Japs." The *Waco Messenger*, the city's black newspaper, described him as "a young man of fine qualities. He possesses commendable poise, a winning presence, and unaffected modesty. His clear magnetic eyes reveal intelligence, sincerity, purpose, courage, and calmness."[14]

Miller briefly returned to Waco on 24 January. There, according to his brother James Arthur, he broke off his engagement to Mozelle Alexander, saying that he did not wish to leave a war widow. "This will be my last roundup," he reportedly told his younger brother. "I won't be back. If the Japanese don't get me, some jealous shipmate will."[15] With regard to the jealousy of his shipmates, historian Leroy Ramsey reported that Miller confided in his older brother, Connery

Jr., that since receiving the Navy Cross "my life is a holy hell. The white folks never did like me because I'm colored. Now the colored guys aboard ship do not like me because they say the I think I'm somebody special."[16]

As for his fear of being killed by the Japanese, his high school friend Pauline Adams later told a reporter for the *Waco Tribune-Herald* that on his last night at home Miller had joined several friends at a nightclub near Lake Waco. While others danced, she and Miller sat at a table and talked until nearly four o'clock in the morning. He told her the story of his Pearl Harbor exploits, but "then, all at once, he started looking real sad." She asked what the matter was, and he replied, "'Don't tell anybody, but when I go back, I'm going on a suicide mission.' And he started crying."[17] It seems wildly improbable that Miller had, in fact, received such an assignment—or, in fact, any assignment at all at that date—and why or whether he actually believed that he had been assigned to a "suicide mission" is impossible now to ascertain, but these statements clearly indicate that Doris Miller was greatly troubled by his imminent return to active duty.

But before he returned to his ship, he had one more public relations duty to perform. Leaving his boyhood home for the last time the next day, Messman Miller took the train north to Chicago, where he was greeted by many of the leading citizens of the city's Southside and where Mayor Edward Kelly presented to him the key to the city. On 28 January 1943 the young sailor addressed the Fraternal Council of Negro Churches in America at the Monumental Baptist Church and attended the ceremony for the first black class to graduate from the US Naval Training Station at Great Lakes. There, in the lounge of the camp's recreation building, hung twelve large murals painted by black navy artists on the theme of "the Negro in the navy." One of those was of Doris Miller, manning a machine gun at Pearl Harbor.

Shortly after cracking the door on black enlistment, Secretary Knox had announced that Negro recruits who volunteered for general service would be trained at the Naval Training Station at Great Lakes, Illinois. Although the recruits that the navy planned to send to Great Lakes would be housed in segregated barracks, black men would be allowed to serve outside of the messman branch.

By 1 June 1942, Camp Robert Smalls at the Great Lakes Naval Training Center was opened to the first 1,000 recruits. After eight weeks of basic training at this all-black advanced-training service school, recruits, for the first time, gained the opportunity to attend a sixteen-week course for gunners, quartermasters, radiomen, and yeomen as well as for cooks and bakers. But despite this apparent step toward equality, the facility maintained many of the navy's traditional racist attitudes and behaviors.[18]

The facility's commandant, Lt. Cmdr. Daniel W. Armstrong, was the son of Brig. Gen. Samuel Chapman Armstrong, who had commanded the Eighth US Colored Infantry during the Civil War, served in the Freedman's Bureau, and in 1878 founded the Hampton Institute in Hampton, Virginia. Even so, in common with most whites and even many of the most idealistic abolitionists, General Armstrong maintained that "it was the duty of the superior white race to rule over the weaker dark-skinned races until they were appropriately civilized." That civilizing process, in Armstrong's estimate, would require several generations of moral and religious development. White civilization could be instilled in African Americans only by the moral power of labor and manual industry, a belief shared and perpetuated at Tuskegee Institute by Booker T. Washington.[19]

General Armstrong's views also permeated those of his son, who believed that blacks should retain their own "culture" and remain "separate" within the total population.[20] In this, Commander Armstrong was in line with the navy's basic policy that separation was necessary because the great majority of white personnel desired it. Abandonment of the policy would adversely affect morale, the navy brass believed, and would result in serious racial conflict.

Black sailors also preferred segregation, the white officers and civilian administrators maintained, as the pattern to which they were long accustomed by civilian experience.

In keeping with Armstrong's view of black culture, he insisted that his sailors sing spirituals on Sunday evenings. He "attempted by this and other means to fix social causation on the importance of the African heritage of Negro[e]s, and to regard it as a sign of the Negro's lack of capacity for higher civilization and learning."[21]

At the ceremony marking the first graduating class from Camp Robert Smalls,[22] Doris Miller was seated on the speakers' platform between Lieutenant Commander Armstrong and retired Brig. Gen. Spencer C. Dickerson, a black hero of World War I. He was introduced by a hero of the battles of the Coral Sea and Midway, R. Adm. Frank Jacob Lowry, then serving as executive officer of the training station, who recounted Miller's heroism at Pearl Harbor, calling him a credit to the navy. "Every one of you men graduating has the opportunity to be singled out for some similar honor during your life in the navy," Lowry affirmed.[23]

Speaking without notes, Miller warned the graduates of the importance of being "on the alert at all times." The keynote of his talk, however, was the tremendous pride he felt in the navy and of the privilege of being a part of it. "It is almost unbelievable just what the perfect co-ordination and strength of our navy actually is," he told a reporter.[24] He urged the new sailors to "take advantage of their opportunities," and he assured the graduates that he was "sure you men have the stuff to make your way in the navy. Take advantage of every opportunity while in training and I'm sure you'll accomplish something later on for which you all will be proud the rest of your lives."[25]

After leaving Chicago, Miller returned to the West Coast where he spent the remainder of the winter on shore duty in Oakland. There he socialized with C. Robert Jenkins, a fellow black naval enlisted man assigned to the USS *Rixey* at the Treasure Island Naval Base. The two men met at the black USO on San Francisco's

Buchanan Street and, according to Jenkins, "became buddies." Miller, Jenkins recalled, "was out to have a good time and didn't talk about Pearl Harbor, [except that] he acknowledged he shot down five or six planes."[26]

Yet Pearl Johns, a reporter for the *Baltimore Afro-American*, wrote, "Dorie Miller is a modest guy. I met him the other night at the colored USO club, which was formerly the Japanese YMCA. I had a long conversation with him and found him a swell person. He has not let success go to his head. He was not wearing his medal and his new stripes. I asked where his other uniform was and he made an excuse that it was at the cleaner's and then winked."[27]

In an interview with E. F. Joseph, a reporter for the *Pittsburgh Courier*, Miller stated that when the Japanese attacked, he "forgot all about the fact that I and other Negroes can be only messmen in the navy and are not taught how to man an antiaircraft gun. . . . Several men had lost their lives—including some of the high officers—when the order came for volunteers from below to come to the upper deck and help fight the Japanese. Without knowing how I did it—it must've been God's strength and my mother's blessing—I ran up only to find that the officers who issued the order had been injured, so another fellow and I started to fire the big guns. And I actually downed four Japanese bombers. I might have brought down more, but I am positive of four."[28]

On 15 May 1943 Miller was reassigned to the Puget Sound Navy Yard at Bremerton, Washington. In June 1943, in one of his infrequent letters to his mother—"He don't write much," she recalled—Miller asked her to "prepare a place at the table for me in 1945. I will eat dinner with you all with a smile." Somewhat cryptically he added, "Tell my friends to live the life that I am living."[29]

At Puget Sound Miller received training as a cook, and on 1 June he was reassigned as an officer's cook, third class.[30] There, too, on the same day, he was reassigned to the newly commissioned escort carrier USS *Liscome Bay*. His new ship was a CVE, a so-called "baby flattop." Only half the length of such fleet carriers as *Enterprise,* escort carriers were relatively slow and much less well armed and armored, but they were also less expensive and more quickly built.[31] All of *Liscome Bay*'s officers and the overwhelming majority of its sailors were white, but the carrier's crew included roughly two dozen messmen.[32]

After training exercises on the West Coast, Miller enjoyed a brief shore leave to visit his older brother, Selvia, who was then working in a defense plant in Los Angeles. *Liscome Bay* departed San Diego on 21 October 1943, arriving at Pearl Harbor one week later. There Miller's ship was attached to R. Adm. Henry Maston Mullinnix's Northern Attack Force, in consort with the battleship *New Mexico* and escort carriers *Coral Sea* and *Corregidor.* This temporary task group had been formed to support Operation Galvanic, the invasion of the Gilbert Islands, the first thrust by the United States into the central Pacific and a major component of the US strategy in the central Pacific theater. Mullinnix's task group departed Pearl Harbor on 10 November as part of Carrier Division 24, a component of Task Force 52—Northern Attack Force—under Adm. Richard K. Turner.

Miller fell under the command of Ens. Francis X. Daily. "He was a big guy," Daily recalled, "but tender as a deer." Miller's primary duty station was the ship's galley, but during general quarters he manned one of the ship's "Kamikaze killer" 20 mm antiaircraft guns. The first time he and his loader, Messman Theodore R. Harris of East Orange, New Jersey, took their positions at the gun, Ensign Daily and about a dozen of his fellow officers gathered behind Miller and Harris, eager to watch the hero of Pearl Harbor. Daily later recalled that Miller "didn't disappoint," as it took only three or four blasts of the 20 mm gun to destroy a target balloon.[33]

After training in Hawaii and in the Gilbert Islands, the campaign began in earnest on 20 November when *Liscome Bay* supported the crucial and bloody Marine landings on Tarawa and Makin Atoll, sending navy dive bombers against Japanese gun emplacements.

Its aircraft provided a major component in the 2,278 action sorties provided by carrier-based planes, which neutralized enemy air bases. Then, with the islands secured, US forces began to retire.

At 5:10 a.m. on 24 November 1943—the day before Thanksgiving—while cruising near Butaritari Island, the ship's lookout shouted, "Christ, here comes a torpedo!" A single torpedo from Cmdr. Sunao Tabata's Japanese submarine *I-175* struck *Liscome Bay* on the starboard side. Miller responded to general quarters by heading to his 20 mm gun position, shipped on the carrier's port side, but a few moments later the ship's aircraft bomb magazine exploded. "We were hit just back of mid-ship" and just aft of the engine compartment, recalled Robert E. Haynes, one of the survivors. "From here on back, everything was instantly gone."[34] Fragments of burning deck and fiery shards of metal rocketed 1,000 feet into the air and rained down on the battleship *New Mexico*, 1,500 yards away.

The thinly armored *Liscome Bay* carried over 200,000 pounds of bombs, which exploded en masse, as did 120,000 gallons of bunker oil, many thousands of gallons of aviation fuel, and countless 20 mm and 40 mm cannon shells. The ship's stern was lifted out of the water, and the whole after section broke quickly into flames and disintegrated. Most of the crew stationed there died instantly. *Liscome Bay* sank within twenty-three minutes. The CVE was indeed, as the sailors sardonically claimed, "Combustible, Vulnerable, and Expendable."

In US naval history, the size of the carrier's casualty list was second only to that of *Arizona* at Pearl Harbor. Only 272 officers and men survived from the crew of over 900. Doris Miller was not among them. Along with two-thirds of the crew, he was listed as "presumed dead."[35]

7

"They Appreciate What I Did"

The Doris Miller Legacy

ᏫᎥᎥᎥᎥᎥᎥᎥᎥᎥᏬ

Dorie Millers of the future will be captains as well as cooks.

—Congresswoman Barbara Jordan of Texas

In a cruel historical twist, Mr. and Mrs. Connery Miller were notified on 7 December 1943 that their son was "Missing in Action," two years to the day after he had enshrined himself with the black community with his heroic actions at Pearl Harbor. His body was never recovered, and on 25 November 1944 Secretary of the Navy James Forrestal announced that Doris Miller was "presumed dead" at twenty-four years of age.[1]

In a 1944 segment of the radio program *Theater of the Imagination*, broadcast from the US Naval Training and Distribution Center at Treasure Island, prominent movie star Orson Welles asked Connery Miller if he did not take comfort in knowing that his son's death was in the cause of freedom and democracy. The fifty-year-old man replied that he found no comfort at all in his son's death, whatever cause he symbolized. "No. Nothing can lessen the pain of losing Doris."[2]

One year later the elder Miller spoke with a reporter for the *Houston Informer*, a black newspaper, about the persistence of racism. "I live in the South," he said, "and don't want to say nothing that's untrue. But I can't see where we've progressed. I am honestly sincere when I say [that] many white people seemingly hate us more since the war."[3]

Further, black men and women who served in the armed forces during World War II had "hoped that the uniform of their country, proudly worn and honorably served might open the door of opportunity so that they could give of themselves without cavil, stint or reservation," Percival Leroy Prattis, an influential black journalist who had served as a battalion sergeant major in the US Army during World War I, declared. "They have found instead that they are victims of a system of discriminatory segregation," imposed by "the iron rule" of the army and navy.[4]

As early as January 1942, the month that saw the inauguration of the "Double V" campaign, President Roosevelt had responded to complaints that ship builders were violating E. O. 8802 by denying black union members employment. In a letter to Joseph Curran, head of the National Maritime Union, the president condemned such discrimination, but the liberal media continued to call him to task for his ongoing sanction of the navy's blatant racism. The day after writing to Curran, therefore, Roosevelt allegedly told Knox, "I think that with all the navy activities, [you] might invent something that colored enlistees could do in addition to the rating of messman."[5]

In the face of such pressure, Knox ordered the navy's general board to devise a plan to recruit 5,000 African Americans for services in general ratings. The board recommended the "experimental" use of blacks in a variety of scenarios under strictly segregated conditions.

Despite these restrictions, the *Pittsburgh Courier*'s editor, Robert L. Vann, saw this as an achievable step on the path toward full integration of the military, but the NAACP leadership, primarily Walter White, publicly disagreed with this half-measure. As a result of the *Courier*'s influence, Congressman Hamilton Fish IV of New York successfully added an amendment prohibiting racial discrimination in the selection and training of men drafted under the Selective Training and Service Act of 1940.[6]

Not until 1944, however, concurrently with the change of policy on assignment of black sailors to general ratings, did the navy issue its "Guide to the Command of Negro Naval Personnel," which stated that "the Navy accepts no theories of racial differences in inborn ability, but expects that every man wearing its uniform be trained and used in accordance with his maximum individual capacity determined on the basis of individual performance." This guide constituted a major step toward President Harry S. Truman's Executive Order 9981, the 1948 directive that mandated "the equality of treatment of opportunity for all those who serve in our country's defense . . . without regard to race, color, religion or national origin," resulting in the desegregation of the armed forces.[7]

Doris Miller's death clearly was not in vain. In 1956 the *Pittsburgh Courier*, which had so long championed Miller's cause, proclaimed that he had "died for his country so that his people might rise another notch in dignity and courage. Every blow struck for civil rights is a monument to Dory Miller, citizen." Historian Richard E. Miller identified him as "the most identifiable enlisted sailor in the battle of Pearl Harbor, if not of the entire Pacific War," and Pulitzer Prize–winner Doris Kearns Goodwin has stated that "the example of Miller's heroism became a principal weapon in the battle to end discrimination in the navy."[8]

African Americans' crucial work in wartime industries and their courageous service in the armed forces—combined with the powerful ideals of American democracy—engendered a new civil rights agenda that forever transformed the nation's life. In 1949 President Harry S. Truman appointed a seven-member Committee on Equality of Treatment and Opportunity, chaired by Charles H. Fahy of Georgia, to oversee the full and permanent integration of the armed forces of the United States. Arguably, this transformation would have been much later in coming had not Doris

Miller demonstrated courage and devotion above and beyond the call of duty of the black sailor at Pearl Harbor. In 1960 the *Courier* credited him with striking a "fatal blow" against "Navy racism" and leaving "ajar the door through which thousands of Negro[e]s have traveled to important Navy posts."[9] Numerous historians believe that Doris Miller's actions at Pearl Harbor helped convince the navy to allow all black sailors roles other than as messmen and that the advances in World War II foreshadowed desegregation of the military in 1948 and the civil rights movement of the 1950s and 1960s. Important as they were, Doris Miller's heroic actions on the day of the Pearl Harbor attack did not sound the death knell of racism in America.

"We can believe that the Negro in war has earned the right to fair and non-discriminatory treatment in time of peace," wrote Joseph S. Roucek, head of the Department of Political and Social Science at Hofstra College, "and that good Americans will recognize this right." But when Paul Jarrico, a Hollywood scriptwriter and producer who was to be blacklisted by Joseph McCarthy's US Senate Foreign Relations subcommittee in 1950, traveled to Waco to interview Connery Miller, he refused to speak in patriotic platitudes. "When black boys and white boys fight and die together," Jarrico asked, "don't you think it makes for a change?" "Could be," the elder Miller replied. "I don't see no change yet."[10]

Doris Miller might have said of the Japanese, as Muhammad Ali said of the Viet Cong, "My conscience won't let me go shoot my brother, or some darker people, or some poor hungry people in the mud for big powerful America. And shoot them for what? They never called me nigger, they never lynched me, they didn't put no dogs on me, they didn't rob me of my nationality, rape and kill my mother and father . . . Shoot them for what? How can I shoot them poor people? Just take me to jail."[11]

Instead, in October 1943, Doris Miller told the editor of the *California Eagle*, "I believe that young Negro[e]s will struggle for their full rights when this war is over. I know I will."[12] Miller died within a month of making that statement, but by 2016 the US Navy had six black admirals, one of whom, Paul Reason, had achieved four-star rank and was commander of the Atlantic Fleet, giving the African American community hope for the future. As black poet and novelist Langston Hughes wrote in 1935,

> I say it plain,
> America never was America to me,
> And yet I swear this oath—America will be![13]

"The numerous retellings since 1942 have inevitably exaggerated the numbers of aircraft shot down and other aspects of the story," observed historian Richard E. Miller, "and careless quasi-historians have perpetuated misconceptions." Shortly before his death, Miller himself made the claim that he and Lieutenant White had shot down four Japanese planes each at Pearl Harbor, and "if we hadn't operated and gotten these planes, they would've submerged the ship entirely." However many Japanese planes he may or may not have shot down, Doris Miller deserves his niche in the pantheon of American heroes as he deserves his Navy Cross, for he provided an immeasurably important symbol for black Americans in their struggle for desegregation and equal opportunity, not only in the armed forces, but throughout the breadth of American society.[14]

As historian Ronald Takaki argued, black Americans insisted that their country live up to its ideals and founding principles, and they went to war "not only for victory over fascism abroad but also for victory over prejudice at home."[15] By helping to defeat the Axis, black Americans realized one-half of the "Double V." The remaining half—a victory over discrimination and segregation in American life—remained elusive. The social, economic, and political gains were often lost with the end of the war—as they had been following the American Revolution, the Civil War, and World War I—contributing to the disillusionment and upheaval of the 1960s, but the American military continued after the war to break down barriers to not only African Americans but to women and minorities generally.

The 26 September 1942 issue of the *Pittsburgh Courier* contained one of Miller's very few letters, written "in behalf of the things that you have done for me in the past, and also for my fellow man, of my standing. For you have opened up things a little for us, at least for the ones who were following me, and I hope it will be better in the near future."[16]

Philip A. Klinkner, a professor of government at Hamilton College, argues that "significant advances in racial justice have occurred only when three circumstances have converged: large-scale wars which require extensive mobilization of African Americans; an enemy that inspires American leaders to advocate egalitarian values in order to justify the war; and domestic political organizations that pressure leaders to follow through on their rhetoric."[17] In 1942, with all of these factors in place, the navy reluctantly agreed to enlist blacks gradually in a wider array of specialties. Yet even then the navy remained adamant about preserving racial segregation aboard its ships. Therefore, two-thirds of the blacks enlisted under the new, more open policy were messmen, and the rest were confined to shore duty and labor jobs, mostly loading and unloading ammunition ships, where they could be more easily segregated.[18]

Beginning in 1944, however, with the replacement of the blatantly racist Franklin Knox with James Forrestal as secretary of the navy, the service relaxed its rigid policies of racial exclusion and segregation, at least to a degree, and blacks were offered significantly greater opportunities. In January 1944 a special all-black navy officers' candidate school opened at the Great Lakes, Illinois, Naval Training Station. These officers, however, were to command only black enlisted men,[19] and the war ended before many of them could see combat. And although commanded by white officers, all-black crews manned the destroyer escort *Mason* and the submarine chaser *PC-1264*.[20]

Childhood memories of her mother telling her about Miller inspired Juliete Parker, a retired mechanical engineer from Detroit, to write *A Man Named Doris*. "It was more of an emotion I caught from her," Parker said. "Her eyes would light up and she would say his name with reverence." This is because, according to historian Philip Klinkner, Miller's story encapsulates the black experience in World War II: "Despite discrimination and maltreatment they rose to the occasion; despite not being able to share in all the blessings of being American, they helped defend their country."[21]

Why, then, asked Professor Lawrence D. Reddick, was Doris Miller not acclaimed a national hero? His story epitomized what Reddick identified as the "classic hero tradition." He was the son of a Texas sharecropper, rising "from obscurity to triumph," standing like a man in the face of danger, and "courageously shot down enemy planes as his captain lay dying on his fatally damaged ship." "All of the drama for a great saga was here," Reddick maintained, and this at a time when the news of the attack on Pearl Harbor had so stunned and dismayed the nation that a hero was sorely needed. "Did Miller's color disqualify him for such a role?"[22]

For black Americans, Doris Miller—as the iconic hero of the war, the "everyman" soldier who performed at the most crucial time, beyond his training, to preserve the nation and rally black support for the war effort—provided a strong platform for challenging segregation. "What he did for his captain, his ship, his service and his country would contribute toward removing the still existing discriminations against Negro[e]s in the sea service," declared the *New York Times*. Miller's sacrifices afforded him a reputation far above his rank and disproved the navy's contention that the alleged stupidity and cowardice of the black man fitted him only for menial duty aboard warships.[23] In the words of an editorial in the *California Eagle*, "Dorie has become a symbol of the patriotism of the Negro." His "simple and heroic story so eloquently illustrated the whole position of the Negro in the U.S. Navy at the time of Pearl Harbor that it was retold a thousand times—retold in the midst of scathing attacks upon the Navy's 'messman only' policy for Negro recruits."[24]

In addition, "thousands of white people have acted as though they appreciate what I did," Miller told a Los Angeles newsman in October 1943. "I feel that the drawing together of Negro[e]s and white people is a good thing coming of the war. I think the unity of the races will continue."[25]

Many whites, indeed, have been inspired by Miller's heroic story. Even conservative icon Ronald Reagan added it to his anthology of classic American tales. In a 1975 speech in North Carolina, the "Great Communicator"—no doubt influenced by a viewing of *Tora! Tora! Tora!*—regaled the crowd with the tale of "a Negro sailor whose total duties involved kitchen-type duties," who shot down four dive bombers with a borrowed machine gun. "He cradled the machine gun in his arms, which is not an easy thing to do, and stood on the end of the pier, blazing away at Japanese planes that were coming down and strafing him." The true import of Miller's bravery was, according to Reagan, that it single-handedly, once and for all, ended racial inequality in America. "When the first bombs were dropped on Pearl Harbor," he said, "there was great segregation in the military forces."[26]

Black opinion as to the hope of racial unity, as expressed by contemporary African American poets, however, remained divided. Some were as sanguine as Reagan. "When Dorie Miller took gun in hand," Langston Hughes wrote in 1943, "Jim Crow started his last stand." And although Hughes admits that "our battle yet is far from won," he is certain that "when it is, Jim Crow'll be done. We gonna bury that son of a gun."[27] In a similar vein, blues singer Josh White expected that the future of race relations would be greatly improved because of the heroics of such black soldiers and sailors as Doris Miller. In a song called "Dorie Miller," which he never recorded, he boasts that "Japan came messin' around, where she didn't have no right" until "they found Dorie Miller, behind that great big Navy gun. He made them wish they'd stayed in the land of the risin' sun." However, even after bestowing upon Miller one of its highest awards, the navy still would not allow him to serve in a combat post, sending him "back to the messroom with the Navy Cross he'd won." In White's opinion, "they should have placed him right back behind that big Navy gun."

> Now if we want to win this war and sink those
>   U-boats in the tide,
> We've got to have black and white sailors fighting
>   side by side.[28]

Much less optimistically, Gwendolyn Brooks's 1945 dramatic monolog, "Negro Hero—to Suggest Dorie Miller," exposes the tenuous and contradictory situation of black sailors in a white man's navy. In her view, Miller's battle was more against racial discrimination at home than it was against the Japanese attackers, and the outcome was still entirely dubious.

Her Doris Miller was certainly a patriot. "I loved," he says, "and a man will guard when he loves." Ironically, though, what he loved was alien and even a danger to him. "Their White-gowned democracy was my fair lady," but that "lady" held a knife "lying cold, straight, in the softness of her sweet-flowing sleeve." Even so, "for the sake of the dear smiling mouth" and for her "stuttered promise" of equality, he risked, and ultimately forfeited, his life. But even then, he asks, "am I clean enough to kill for them," and, more important, "am I good enough to die for them, is my blood bright enough to be spilled" in defense of white America, "or is my place in the galley still?" His answer, the most powerful line in Brooks's poem, is that

> I helped to save them,
> them and a part of their democracy,
> Even if I had to kick their law into their teeth in
>   order to do that for them.

Brooks's Miller believed that he had done a good job, but the "possible horror" remained: that white America might not want to be saved by black heroism and sacrifice, "that they might prefer the preservation of their law in all its sick dignity and their knives to the continuation of their creed and their lives."[29]

Although in 1969 *Ebony* magazine described Miller as "all-but-forgotten," he remained firmly in the collective memory of the black community.[30] And although famed black Texas congress-woman Barbara Jordan ruefully noted that "for a period of time, it appeared the navy had forgotten about Dorie Miller," public tributes to the heroic messman have been numerous and continuing. Not only was he the first African American to be awarded the Navy Cross, his acts were heavily publicized in the black press, making him black America's "number one hero"—thereby energizing black support for the war effort against fascism and sustaining African American pride and patriotism.[31]

The first of many remembrances was a memorial service sponsored by the Victory Club, held on 30 April 1944 at Waco's Second Baptist Church, and on 28 May 1944 a granite marker was dedicated at A. J. Moore High School. Also in his hometown a cemetery, the Doris Miller Memorial Park, bears his name as does a branch of the YMCA. At its dedication in February 1994, James Miller, the president of the Waco chapter of Concerned Black Citizens, remarked that "we are looking for some positive role models for our young people. It's good to know that young people will see this marker every day and will be able to learn about Doris Miller and what he did for America."[32] The Bledsoe-Miller Community Center, a community recreation facility, was jointly named for Doris Miller and Jules Bledsoe, another Waco native, who studied medicine at Columbia University and won fame as a classical musician.[33]

Waco's Doris Miller Elementary School, now closed, also bore his name. The Doris Miller Department of Veterans Affairs Medical Center, with its monument to Miller and a street named Doris

Miller Drive, was dedicated in 1984. And most recently, on 7 December 2016, Waco dedicated the two-acre Miller Memorial Park on the banks of the Brazos River, featuring a $1.35 million park and public art installation created by architect Stan Carroll and sculptor Eddie Dixon. The design consists of a stylized 170-foot-by-30-foot ship's hull displaying the salient events of Miller's life, and a 9-foot statue of Miller himself overlooking a reflecting pool.

Elsewhere in Texas, the American Legion's Post 817 in Beaumont is named in his honor, and on 10 December 1992 a shopping center in San Antonio, which served as a recreational area, police department outpost, and social service agency, is named the Dorie Miller Center. An auditorium on the campus of Huston-Tillotson College in Austin is dedicated to his memory, and elementary schools in Houston and in San Antonio, an intermediate school in Ennis, and a junior high school in San Marcos serve as symbols "of what Miller fought and died for." In the words of the principal of the San Antonio school, "He will live long in the hearts and minds of the youngsters who will pass through the doors of this institution."[34]

Elementary schools also bear his name in Philadelphia and in San Diego, as does a Veterans of Foreign Wars chapter in Los Angeles. On 11 October 1991 the Alpha Kappa Alpha sorority dedicated a bronze commemorative plaque at the Miller Family Park, located on the US Naval Base, Pearl Harbor. A housing community in Gary, Indiana, a community center in Newport News, Virginia, an American Legion post in Chicago, a Disabled American Veterans Chapter in Washington, DC, a park in Lewisburg, West Virginia, and a street in Champaign, Illinois, are all Miller's namesakes.[35] And in December 1953 black congressman Adam Clayton Powell dedicated the Dorie Miller Housing Project, a $2.7 million housing cooperative in the Corona neighborhood of New York City with these words: "It is fitting that New York's first unsegregated cooperative housing project should be named after the first hero who fought at Pearl Harbor."[36]

Chicago's Doris Miller Foundation, established in 1947 by Reverend Elmer L. Fowler of Chicago's Third Baptist Church, perpetuates Miller's memory by honoring individuals and organizations promoting "the progress, welfare and prestige of American citizens of the black race." Among its recipients have been Jackie Robinson, Mary McCleod Bethune, Medgar Evers, John F. Kennedy, and Aretha Franklin.[37] And in 1950 the Dorie Miller Trophy was presented to the entire personnel of the US Navy for outstanding work in race relations. Secretary of the Navy Francis P. Matthews accepted the trophy for the navy "with profound gratefulness and with pride in the occasion which prompts the ceremony." Matthews praised Miller as "a real American, a great American, and a great American hero," adding that "the navy was particularly proud that he belonged to the navy" and that he "honored the navy with his service by his patriotism and devotion to his country."[38]

On 25 April 1944, Canada Lee and Josh White starred in Norman Corwin's production of "Dorie Got a Medal," a drama broadcast on the CBS radio series *Columbia Presents Corwin*, and on 9 December 1945 the ABC radio series *Orson Welles Commentaries* presented a tribute to Miller. During the program Welles announced the naming of the 1,500-seat Theatre One at the Treasure Island Naval Base Theatre Complex to honor Miller.[39]

In addition, Miller was the subject of a 1943 US Navy recruiting poster—"Above and Beyond the Call of Duty"—designed by the famed illustrator David Stone Martin. In February 2010 the US Postal Service issued a set of commemorative stamps featuring Miller as one of four "Distinguished Sailors" recognized for serving with "bravery and distinction." The three others were all senior officers and white.[40]

"History has swept forward through epic times since the morning of December 7," wrote a reporter for the *California Eagle* in October 1943. "But of all the hero stories of that tragic occasion, Dorie Miller's will survive, for in it was found more than a tale

of individual courage. In it was seen the symbol of a great injustice."[41] Even so, the movie industry has been ambiguous toward the black hero. According to one possibly apocryphal story,
Henrietta Miller denied one Hollywood filmmaker permission
to dramatize her son's life when the producer insisted that Doris
Miller be portrayed by a white actor.[42] He did, however, feature
indirectly in such government-sponsored films as John Ford's
1943 feature, *December 7th*, and in the 1944 movie *The Negro
Soldier*, which ends with a pseudo-documentary reenactment
of Miller's heroism at Pearl Harbor. According to film historian
Thomas Cripps, the scene depicts the Roosevelt administration's
"wished-for black dedication to the war and a repudiation of Japanese racial propaganda." In Fox's 1943 film *Crash Dive*, Miller's
persona is, through the magic of Hollywood, transferred to a
submarine where he is portrayed by actor Ben Carter—who had
played the role of an obliging house servant in *Gone with the
Wind*—as "a heroic attendant, very much part of the plot, a fighting man among fighting men."[43]

Thereafter, Miller did not appear on film until 1970, with the
production of *Tora! Tora! Tora!* in which, although not identified
by a name, he was portrayed by Elven Havard. Even then, he is
on screen only momentarily before abandoning his machine gun
and jumping overboard. He next appeared on screen in Michael
Bay's 2001 film, *Pearl Harbor,* which the *New York Times* film critic described as "defiantly, extravagantly average." Portrayed by
Cuba Gooding Jr., Miller enjoyed a somewhat more substantial
appearance.[44]

Despite Doris Miller's continuing fame and numerous com-
memorations, the ultimate award has yet eluded him. Not one
of the 432 Congressional Medals of Honor awarded for service
in World War II went to any of the 1.7 million African American
soldiers and sailors who served, but many admirers believe Miller
to be the best qualified as well as the most popular aspirant for
the award. Although the resolutions of Congressman James Mead

and Senator John Dingell died in committee during the war, many advocates since have petitioned for Miller to receive the Medal of Honor for his acts on 7 December 1941. In fact, James E. Nierle, the president of the Navy Department's Board of Decorations and Medals, has acknowledged that "this case has received more attention than any other award in the Navy's history. Beginning in 1942, and continuing to the present, countless requests have been made to award Doris Miller the Medal of Honor."[45]

Writing about black messmen, "No one expected them to do anything but wash dishes and polish those officers' shoes," said Marion "Tumbleweed" Beach, an African American poet, teacher, and activist from Chicago who has worked since 1944 to secure Miller the Medal of Honor. In March 1964 Rev. Elmer L. Fowler recommended to President Lyndon B. Johnson that Miller be awarded the medal, but the request was denied, although Johnson's military aide did point out that the decision "in no way detracts from his performance" at Pearl Harbor and that the Navy Cross, "awarded only for exceptional heroism in combat," was appropriate and just. In 1987 black congressman Mickey Leland, a Texas Democrat who succeeded Barbara Jordan in representing an inner-city Houston congressional district, advanced a bill to gain Miller the Medal of Honor, but it, too, failed.

On 30 March 1999, Ross L. Fowler, a retired Coast Guard commander from Detroit, forwarded to President William Jefferson Clinton the citations for a number of white recipients of the Medal of Honor, both officers and enlisted personnel, including those who survived the attack on Pearl Harbor and those to whom the medal was awarded posthumously. In all cases, Fowler maintained, the navy had displayed "a blatant discriminatory attitude toward Negroes" and Doris Miller's deeds "surpassed those who did receive the medal." Fowler maintained that Miller was denied the Medal of Honor because it would have required every officer and enlisted man he encountered to salute this black messman.[46]

Emerson Emory of Dallas—a World War II veteran, a doctor of

internal medicine as well as a psychiatrist, and a captain in the US Naval Reserve—waged a personal crusade to have Miller awarded the Medal of Honor, noting that the citation that accompanied Miller's Navy Cross "more than met the criteria for the Medal of Honor" when compared to the citations of various white naval personnel who were so honored. "The only answer to why is— racism additionally overt bigotry."[47]

In 1995 Senator Carol Mosley Braun of Illinois advanced similar legislation in the Senate, and Representatives Chet Edwards and Eddie Bernice Johnson, both of Texas, with the support of Representative John D. Dingell, the Congressional Black Caucus, and several other members, introduced House Resolution 4851 to waive the statute of limitations so that Miller could receive the Medal of Honor, "a long awaited honor."[48]

In a bitterly ironic response, the Bureau of Naval Personnel announced that Asian Americans and Native American Pacific Islanders who had been awarded the Distinguished Service Cross or the Navy Cross during World War II might have their medals upgraded to the Medal of Honor, but African Americans in similar circumstances were excluded from the ruling. Members of the African American community were, of course, further outraged by the pointed exclusion of black veterans from the ruling and the apparent continuation of what one of Charles Hamilton Houston's former law students, Supreme Court justice Thurgood Marshall, labeled the "blatant discriminatory attitude toward Negroes during World War II."[49]

Among Miller's other champions have been Jake Pickle, the longtime Democratic congressman from Central Texas, and Barbara Jordan, the first Southern black woman elected to the US House of Representatives. Most recently, Representative Eddie Bernice Johnson, a Dallas Democrat, formed a committee of Miller's supporters to advocate for the upgrade of his medal to the president, the secretary of the navy, and members of Congress. "We're not stopping," Johnson said. "We are not giving up. It's not my nature to give up on anything I believe in." She has, in fact, taken up Miller's cause with every naval secretary who has served since she arrived in Congress in 1993.[50]

Not until 1997 were seven black veterans awarded the medal that, according to President Bill Clinton, was "the tribute that has always been their due." On 27 October 1988, Under Secretary of the Navy Henry Lawrence Garrett III instructed the Navy Board of Decorations and Medals to conduct a study to determine the extent to which "racial discrimination might have influenced the award of the Medal of Honor" to black sailors. As a result of a similar study in the army, in 1997, President Clinton awarded the medal to seven black soldiers, all but one posthumously. "History has been made whole today," the president said in a White House ceremony. "Today, these injustices are behind us."[51]

The navy's study, however, found no cause for similar action in Miller's case or that of any other sailor.[52] Instead, the navy concluded that the Navy Cross "appropriately recognizes Petty Officer Miller's heroic actions," a navy spokesman said. As the Board of Decorations and Medals explained in response to the 1997 request of Hawaii senator Daniel K. Inouye—himself a Medal of Honor winner—that Miller's Navy Cross be upgraded: "Official reviews of the case have consistently found no evidence that would meet the high standard for requesting upgrade to the Medal of Honor. If new evidence is presented in the future, the Navy will of course accord it all the attention it deserves."[53]

But to Congresswoman Eddie Bernice Johnson, "It is impossible to entirely extract race from consideration of Miller's case. His performance was so extraordinarily above and beyond the call of duty in part because that call was so colored by his race."[54]

"We're still on a mission to get him that medal," said Juliete Parker, author of *A Man Called Doris*, a Miller biography,[55] and as recently as June 2015 Carl Sherman, the mayor of DeSoto, Texas, took the opportunity to urge President Barak Obama to award Miller the Medal of Honor. Their encounter took place at a meeting of the US Conference of Mayors in San Francisco. President Obama promised that he would "seriously consider it," but nothing resulted.[56]

But the navy has found other ways to pay Miller significant tribute. On 30 June 1973 Henrietta Miller christened the USS *Doris Miller* (DE-1091), a *Knox*-class frigate, named for her distinguished son.[57] In her commissioning address that day, Congresswoman Barbara Jordan noted that the launching acknowledged the "contributions of hundreds of black Americans like him to the safety and success of this nation." Congresswoman Jordan reminded her audience, "We cannot forget that we are part of a living experiment, an experiment in democracy. This nation was founded on unprecedented principles of freedom, equality and brotherhood," principles that Americans must defend against attack "from outside our borders and from within." The nation, she maintained, has "made great strides in perfecting the American experiment since Doris Miller first wore the Navy blue and white. In the last two turbulent decades, new guarantees of old long-promised freedoms have been enacted into law." But the process had been difficult, and, she said, "it is by no means over."

The navy, in particular, had experienced dramatic change in recent years in its quest to achieve equality of opportunity, and Jordan expressed confidence that it would continue to strive toward that goal. The service was "shaking free of past reflections of society's prejudices and making equality of opportunities a reality," she said, thus making the christening "a time of pride for black people, and we need pride at this time." Young men and women from minority groups, she continued, "are finding a Navy where the Doris Millers of the future will be captains as well as cooks. The USS *Miller* signals the Navy's determination to recognize merit and performance without regard to race." Further, the new frigate would be a symbol to all the world that the United States "is more and more a colorblind society where people from diverse backgrounds are joined in equality in a great undertaking."[58]

Sadly, *Miller*'s naval career proved less heroic than that of its namesake. Although his brother Arthur stated that "we felt real good" about the naming of the ship in Doris Miller's honor because "We felt like it was something that would last," in January 1982 the frigate was transferred to the Naval Reserve Force. USS *Miller* was decommissioned in 1991 and, on 19 August 1999, transferred to the Turkish navy, where it was cannibalized for spare parts. By 2001 it had been dismantled and was being used as a target in a live missile firing exercise.[59]

In addition to the warship, the navy has dedicated Doris Miller Park, a housing community for junior enlisted men at Pearl Harbor, the dining hall at the Chase Field Naval Air Station in Beeville, Texas,[60] and the Doris Miller Dining Hall at the Great Lakes Recruit Training Center, where he had addressed the first graduating class in 1943. There, too, the bachelor enlisted quarters was dedicated to Miller's memory.[61] At the dedication ceremony on 7 December 1971, Herbert G. Odom, a retired sailor then employed as an instructor at the facility's Electronics Technical School, was the keynote speaker. Odom, like Miller, was the son of black sharecroppers who had joined the navy out of financial necessity during the 1930s. The two men had become friends while stationed at Pearl Harbor, although Odom was attached to the submarine service. Choosing as his theme the racism evident in the navy during those years, Odom told the audience that Miller had "entered the Naval service at a time when the virus of racism was still running rampant. It was the time when the black enlistees were relegated exclusively to the duties of mess attendants. Blacks," he said, "were unable to use arms, but watched the white participants who knew how."[62]

R. Adm. Draper Laurence Kaufmann—himself a winner of the Navy Cross and former superintendent of the US Naval Academy —pledged that "the dedication of this building is just the beginning. Much more important is that we dedicate ourselves to the elimination of discrimination and prejudice between the two great communities in America today."[63]

In 1946 black historian Lawrence D. Reddick spoke of the "great distance between the *then* of Pearl Harbor and the *now* of today," citing reforms toward which he considered Miller's contribution "highly important." By the end of the war, many of the old-line admirals had begun to take official pride in the navy's efforts to rid itself of its racist past, and according to Reddick, "navy policy was based on the principal of integration," with new navy secretary James V. Forestall announcing that "in their attitude, and day to day conduct of their affairs, naval officers and enlisted men shall adhere rigidly and impartially to naval regulations in which no distinction is made between individuals wearing naval uniform, or the uniform of any of the armed services of the United States because of race or color."[64]

In 1951 Secretary of the Navy Francis P. Matthews announced that "the navy is especially proud of its long history of successful integration of its personnel from the newest seaman up through the ranks." The new navy "must not be a party to racial or partisan developments by incident or accident by racial or other group-ings," he wrote, vowing that the Navy Department would continue "the work of eliminating discrimination and providing equal opportunities."

At a memorial service for Doris Miller, held at the Texas State Capitol in May 2001, navy captain Charlie Jones, himself a black man, observed, "Today's sailors are limited only by their drive and initiative to succeed. I thank God for men like Doris Miller and the sacrifices they made. I'm here because of them."[65]

Lawrence Reddick perhaps overstated Miller's influence, however, when he wrote that without his "impulse and thrust" the Jim Crow navy would not have changed. Segregation remained widespread well into the Korean War, and the steward's branch remained exclusively nonwhite. President Harry S. Truman ended the segregation of the armed forces before the Korean War, yet problems persisted. The president's desegregation order had no immediate effect for black soldiers and sailors because the generals and admirals—as a class, social conservatives—found ways to impede its implementation. Not until the 1970s did a new chief of naval operations, Adm. Elmo Zumwalt—himself the 1975 recipient of the Miller Foundation award for "his progressive, equal opportunity programs within the U.S. Navy"—bring an end to what he called "lily-white racist Navy" practices.[66]

But the legacy of the Korean War and the Vietnam War was, in some ways, no less disheartening for black soldiers than the legacy of World War I or World War II. True, the armed forces were, by then, desegregated, and service opened more opportunities for advancement by black Americans. But, as Dr. Martin Luther King stated in a sermon at Riverside Church on 4 April 1967, US hypocrisy in Vietnam dashed the hopes of the poor at home while sending their sons, brothers, and husbands to fight and die in highly disproportionate numbers 8,000 miles away "to guarantee liberties in Southeast Asia which they had not found in southwest Georgia and East Harlem."[67]

Others felt the same. The fiery black activist Stokely Carmichael told a Seattle crowd in 1967 that any black man who fought in a white man's war "was a fool! He should have been fighting white folks instead of dying for white folks!" "So here come World War II," he declaimed, "and we gonna fight! We gonna prove how good we are! Let us fight on the front lines! Let us stop this war! We must fight! We're good Americans!" Black men "gave their lives in Poland to stop Hitler from running over the Poles," but having done so, in 1966 "a Polish honky in Cicero gonna throw a rock at us and tell us to get out of his neighborhood."[68]

Perhaps foremost among disenchanted African Americans was Doris Miller's mother. When her efforts to obtain federal assistance in renovating her home were denied, she complained, "We've been exploited like everything by blacks and whites in the name of

Doris," she told an interviewer. "I think it's awful, because I hear they're supposed to help the family of a son who died a hero fighting for his country."[69]

Yet Doris Miller's heroic actions at Pearl Harbor, and his quiet but persuasive voice as an advocate for positive change, constituted a vital contribution toward the full and equal acceptance of black men and women in the US Navy and the nation that it serves.

Although some historians have argued that "the legitimization and expansion of Jim Crow" during the Second World War set back the timetable for national desegregation,[70] it may with equal legitimacy be said that the war "set the stage for the protracted drama of the civil rights movement and the black revolution that began a decade later,"[71] and that Doris Miller's selfless heroism at Pearl Harbor—and the press attention that it inspired—developed in Congress and in the armed services a greater awareness and sensitivity to the attitudes, talents, aspirations, and loyalties of black men and women to their country.

Notes

⊙‴‴⊙

Epigraph

1. "Oh, What a Time" (author unknown), quoted in Reagon, "World War II Reflected in Black Music," 173.

2. Belle S. Vankin, "Epitaph to My Son, Michael," *XIX Corps Scroll*, no. 3 (24 June 1945), published by the US Army in occupied Germany, copy in Lamar Richard Papers, Eisenhower Center for American Studies.

Preface

3. Cagle, "Cinema: Pearl Harbor's Top Gun," 69.

4. Kilpatrick, *The Southern Case for School Segregation*, 24.

Chapter 1

1. Douglass, *Life and Times of Frederick Douglass*, 414. Ironically, blacks who served as messmen in the US Navy were not granted the privilege of wearing the regulation navy uniform button bearing the traditional anchor motif.

2. Du Bois, "Close Ranks," 111.

3. Chauncey quoted in Mackenzie, *Life of Commodore Oliver Hazard Perry*, 1:186–87.

4. "Negroes in the Navy," 241.

5. Quoted in Altoff, *Amongst My Best Men*, 22.

6. Quoted in Bruce E. Prum, "Where We Stand: A Study of Integration in the U.S. Armed Forces," MS thesis, United States Navy Post Graduate School, Monterey, CA, 1964, 20–21.

7. Letter from "Young Neptune," *Toledo Daily Commercial*, 14 July 1863, quoted in Cotham, *Southern Journey of a Civil War Marine*, 203; US Naval War Records Office, *Official Records of the Union and Confederate Navies in the War of the Rebellion* (hereafter cited as *O.R.N.*), ser. 1, vol. 20, 174, 322, 395–96; Bennett, *Union Jacks*, 159–62.

8. Gideon Welles to David G. Farragut, US Naval War Records Office, *O.R.N.*, ser. 1, vol. 17, 269; Ringle, *Life in Mr. Lincoln's Navy*; Bolster, *Black*

Jacks; Selfridge, *What Finer Tradition*; Harrod, *Manning the New Navy*.

9. US Naval War Records Office, *O.R.N.*, ser. 1, vol. 17, 269.

10. Ibid., ser. 1, vol. 7, 26–27.

11. Quoted in David L. Valuska, "The Negro in the Union Navy, 1861–1865," PhD diss., Lehigh University, 1973, 76.

12. Letter from "Young Neptune," quoted in Cotham, *Southern Journey of a Civil War Marine*, 203; US Naval War Records Office, *O.R.N.*, ser. 1, vol. 20, 174, 322, 395–96; Bennett, *Union Jacks*, 159–65.

13. Ringle, *Life in Mr. Lincoln's Navy*, 15.

14. Hayward "Woody" Farrar, "The Black Soldier in Two World Wars," in Hornsby, *Companion to African American History*, 351, 354.

15. Quoted in Astor, *Right to Fight*, 158.

16. Nalty, *Strength for the Fight*, 83–84.

17. Du Bois, "Returning Soldiers," 13–14.

18. Quoted in James L. Conyers Jr., ed., *Charles H. Houston: An Interdisciplinary Study of Civil Rights Leadership* (Lanham, MD: Lexington Books, 2012), 104. See also Williams, *Eyes on the Prize*, 2–18.

19. Radford, *African-American Heritage in Waco, Texas*, 251.

20. In 1917, forty men of the Twenty-Fourth (Colored) United States Infantry were court-martialed on charges of mutiny for their participation in a riot in Houston. Eighteen were summarily hanged on orders from the camp commandant. Between the years 1880 and 1930, nearly 5,000 Americans were lynched. Of this number, 3,344 were black, and at least 500 were murdered in Texas. C. Calvin Smith, "The Houston Riot of 1917," in Glasrud, *Anti-Black Violence in Twentieth-Century Texas*, 66–83; Farrar, "The Black Soldier in Two World Wars," 354.

21. Foner, *Blacks and the Military in American History*, 129–31.

22. Quoted in Booker, "From Messman to Pearl Harbor Hero."

23. Langley, *Social Reform in the United States Navy*, 61–64; Ronald G. Walters, *American Reformers, 1815–1860* (New York: Hill and Wang, 1978), 37; Nelson, *Integration of the Negro*, 8; Miller, *Messman Chronicles*, 6; Nalty, *Long Passage to Korea*.

24. Quoted in Astor, *Right to Fight*, 158; Not surprisingly, then, at the time of Pearl Harbor attack, the navy's ranks contained only slightly more than 4,000 African Americans. By August 1945, 166,915 blacks—4.5 percent of the total personnel—were in naval service. Dennis D. Nelson, "The Integration of the Negro into the U.S. Navy, 1776–1947," MA thesis, Howard University, 1947, 1–2; Farrar, "The Black Soldier in Two World Wars," 351, 354; Nelson, *Integration of the Negro into the U.S. Navy*, 11–12.

25. Knox quoted in President's Committee on Equality of Treatment and Opportunity in the Armed Services, *Freedom to Serve*, 17. See also Haynes, *Awesome Power*, 88.

26. Nelson, *Integration of the Negro*, 13.

27. The *Pittsburgh Courier,* an African American newspaper published in Pittsburgh, Pennsylvania, from 1907 until 22 October 1966, was, by the 1930s, one of the most influential black newspapers in the United States. Buni, *Robert L. Vann*; Finkle, *Forum for Protest*.

28. Quoted in Astor, *Right to Fight*, 158.

29. Ibid.; Miller, *Messman Chronicles*, 130.

30. *Pittsburgh Courier,* 21 December 1940, quoted in Wynn, *Afro-American and the Second World War*, 22.

Chapter 2

1. Some sources place the Miller home near Speegleville, eight miles west of Waco in central McLennan County. The Speegleville post office operated until 1929 when construction of Waco Dam on the Bosque River drove some residents from their homes. A second dam, completed in the 1960s, completely inundated the original townsite. Sharon Bracken, ed., *Historic McLennan County: An Illustrated History* (San Antonio, TX: Historical Publishing Network, 2011), n.p. In a 1971 interview with Thomas E. Turner, a former Baylor University administrator and amateur historian, Henrietta Miller spelled her husband's name as Conery, with only a single *n*. Henrietta Miller, interview by Thomas E. Turner Sr., September 1971, Thomas E. Turner Sr. Papers, box 104, "Doris Miller" folder, Texas Collection, Baylor University.

2. Interview with Arthur J. Miller, 21 March 1971, quoted in Lynn Flematti, "Doris Miller: War Hero," term paper, Baylor University, 2 April 1979, 1. Original in Doris Miller Vertical File, Baylor University Library. Henrietta Miller, interview by Turner, Thomas E. Turner Sr. Papers.

3. Interview with Arthur Miller, quoted in Flematti, "Doris Miller: War Hero," 1.

4. Quoted in Adams, "From Squirrels to Bombers," 1A.

5. Quoted in Duty, "Waco at the Turn of the Century," 2–3; Carver, *Brann and the Iconoclast*.

6. "Mighty Spectacle Is Birth of a Nation," *Waco Times-Herald*, 12 November 1915, 4; "The Late Unpleasantness," *Temple Daily Telegram*, 4 August 1915; *Iconoclast*, quoted in Carver, *Brann and the Iconoclast*, 43–44. See also Bernstein, *First Waco Horror,* 79–80.

7. Connery Miller quoted in "Son Died in Vain, Says Dorie Miller's Father," *Baltimore Afro-American*, 15 December 1945, 1, 19. Copeland, "Doris Miller Stamp Presented in Waco before Packed House." Henrietta Miller quoted in "Mrs. Miller Is Guest Speaker on 'Wings' Program over KTRH," *Dallas Express*, 16 May 1942, 1; "I Had to Spank Doris to Make Him Protect Himself," *Pittsburgh Courier*, 14 May 1942, 4.

Doris Miller's three brothers were Selvia, Connery Jr., and Arthur James. Although some sources indicate that all three brothers were drafted into the army, better evidence suggests that Connery Jr. served in the US Army during World War II while Selvia worked in the defense industry in California. Arthur James, the youngest, remained at home with his parents. Connery and Henrietta Miller were the grandparents of fourteen children, one of whom, Selvia "Junior" Miller, was an All-American tight end for the Nebraska Cornhuskers in the 1970s and for the Atlanta Falcons and New Orleans Saints of the National Football League in the early 1980s, during which time he played twice in the Pro Bowl. Svendsen, "Wacoans Recall Hero's Bravery during Pearl Harbor Attack," 2B; "Mrs. Henrietta Miller," *Waco Tribune-Herald*, 10 June 1982, 10D; "Honors Due for Waco Parents of Negro War Hero," *Waco Herald-Tribune*, 5 April 1942.

Miller's birthplace and childhood home was inundated in 1965 with the damming of the Bosque River west of the city of Waco and the impoundment of Lake Waco as a reservoir and flood control facility. Radford, *African-American Heritage in Waco, Texas*, 251; Kenneth Hendrickson Jr., *The Waters of the Brazos: A History of the Brazos River Authority, 1929–1979* (Waco: Texian Press, 1981).

8. Quoted in Little, "Doris Miller Made Presence Felt."

9. Gregory, "Home of the Brave," 32–34.

10. Copeland, "Doris Miller Stamp Presented in Waco." A. J. Moore High School, located at 600 South First Street, was constructed in 1881, and its first class graduated in 1896. Originally a four-room frame building, it acquired several additional rooms in 1900, and in 1916 an industrial building of three rooms was constructed on the campus. The main building burned in 1921 and was replaced in 1923 by a brick building of twenty-one classrooms, a library, and a cafeteria. Radford, *African-American Heritage in Waco, Texas*, 67–68.

11. Quoted in Adams, "From Squirrels to Bombers," 1A.

12. Quoted in Smith, "Austin Service Celebrates Doris Miller," 3B.

13. Quoted in Smith, "Valor at Sunrise," A12.

14. Quoted in Adams, "From Squirrels to Bombers," 10A.

15. Quoted in Lee, *1941: Texas Goes to War*, 123. In another interview, Henrietta Miller stated, "Things was tight, you know. Wasn't much work to do." Henrietta Miller, interview by Turner, Thomas E. Turner Sr. Papers.

16. Quoted in Adams, "From Squirrels to Bombers," 10A.

17. Ibid.; Joyner, "Rethinking the Recognition of Doris Miller."

18. Naval History and Heritage Command, "The African American Experience in the U.S. Navy: Transcript of Service, Cook Third Class Doris Miller, USN," https://www.history.navy.mil/browse-by-topic/diversity/african-americans/miller/transcript-of-service.html. Mouzon quoted in Miller, *Messman Chronicles*, 287–88.

19. Quoted in Joyner, "Rethinking the Recognition of Doris Miller," n.p.

20. Quoted in Miller, *Messman Chronicles*, 287–88.

21. Smith, *Mountain State Battleship*.

22. Quoted in Lang, "Dorie Miller Was a Hero."

23. The source of this information, Nelson, *Integration of the Negro*, 23–24, can be faulted for misinformation. Doris Miller, for example, was, according to this source, assigned to the battleship *Arizona* during the attack on Pearl Harbor, and his battle station was "on the bridge near the commanding officer, Captain Franklin Van Valkinbergh [i.e., Van Valkenburgh]," who was, in fact, the commander of *Arizona*.

24. Lord, *Day of Infamy*, 52–53.

Chapter 3

1. Brooks, "Negro Hero—to Suggest Dorie Miller," 44–45.

2. Hardwick Thompson, interview by Juliete Parker, 12 February 1989, quoted in Parker, *A Man Named Doris*, 31. F.C. Joe Paul, interview by Juliete Parker, 3 August 1996, quoted in ibid.

3. Quoted in Smith, "Valor at Sunrise," A1.

4. Delano quoted in Grady, "Remembering an American Hero," n.p. Clark Simmons, who was a mess attendant on USS *Utah* during the Pearl Harbor attack, later made the statement that *West Virginia*'s "captain and the executive officer, the 'XO,' were on the bridge and they both were injured." He was also confused in his belief that Miller "physically picked up the captain and brought him down to the first-aid station." Other sources state that Bennion's wound was caused by a bomb fragment, a .50 caliber shell, or a flying piece of *Arizona*'s bridge. Simmons quoted in *National Geographic*, "Beyond the Movie: Pearl Harbor," n.p.

5. Joseph, "'I Downed Four Enemy Planes,'" 1.

6. Johnson quoted in Aiken, "Doris Miller and His Navy Cross," n.p.

7. As Lt. (j.g.) Frederick H. White described the captain's wound, his "abdomen was cut apparently by a fragment of bomb, about three by four inches, with part of his intestines protruding." Quoted in Miller, *Messman Chronicles*, 292–93; see also White, "Statement of Japanese Attack on December 7, 1941." Delano quoted in Grady, "Remembering an American Hero," n.p.

8. White was even taller than Miller, with size 14EEE shoes, which gave him the nickname "Mr. Snowshoes." White, "Statement of Japanese Attack on December 7, 1941."

9. *West Virginia* was refloated and repaired and in 1944 rejoined the war against Japan.

10. White, "Statement of Japanese Attack on December 7, 1941."

11. Quoted in Cutler, *Sailor's History*, n.p.

12. Lord, *Day of Infamy*, 131–32; Prange, *At Dawn We Slept*, 524–25; Levin, "Doris Miller's War."

13. Joseph, "'I Downed Four Enemy Planes,'" 1; Levin, "For the Sailor's Honor"; Prange, *At Dawn We Slept*, 514–15; White, "Statement of Japanese Attack on December 7, 1941"; Howarth, *To Shining Sea*, 382–93.

14. "Christmas 1942," typescript transcription of unidentified newspaper article, in possession of authors.

15. Joseph, "'I Downed Four Enemy Planes,'" 1.

16. Quoted in Miller, *Messman Chronicles*, 292–93.

17. Lord, *Day of Infamy*, 134; Aiken, "Doris Miller and His Navy Cross."

18. Quoted in Aiken, "Doris Miller and His Navy Cross," n.p.

19. Beal quoted in ibid., n.p. Miller's niece, Vickie Gail Miller, an author of children's books, repeats a bit of family lore in her biography of her uncle: "He aimed at one Japanese plane and fired. His first round of rapid fire was a precise hit. The plane crashed into the harbor, plunging head first. It barely escaped the deck of the *West Virginia*." Miller, *Doris Miller*, 49–50.

20. Karig, *Battle Report*, 73.

21. Doris Miller was not the only black messman firing an antiaircraft gun on that day. Aboard the destroyer USS *Ramsay*, his friend Hardwick Thompson was also blasting away with a machine gun. Early in the battle *Ramsay* had made a break for open water and was the second US ship to clear Pearl Harbor. As it steamed past the disabled and capsized *Ogallala*, Thompson had the eerie recognition that this was the ship on which he had so recently been incarcerated, and were he still in the ship's brig, he would have been trapped below and drowned. Thompson, interview by Parker, quoted in Parker, *A Man Named Doris*, 49.

22. R. H. Hillenkoetter to Commander-in-Chief, Pacific Fleet, "Action of December 7, 1941—Report of," 11 December 1941, http://www.usswestvirginia.org/battle_report.htm.

23. All eight battleships of the US Pacific Fleet were sunk or badly damaged, but seven of them—excluding *Arizona*—were eventually raised, and six were deployed in World War II battles. On 17 May 1942, *West Virginia* was salvaged from the seabed by draining the water from its hull. Refloated, repaired, and modernized, the battleship served in the Pacific theater to the end of the war in August 1945. Amazingly, all of the US aircraft carriers were untouched.

24. Quoted in Miller, *Messman Chronicles*, 292–93; Ramsey, "Medal of Honor," 5A.

25. Miller, *Doris Miller*, 57.

26. Smith, "Valor at Sunrise," A12.

27. Ibid., A1.

28. Quoted in Joseph, "'I Downed Four Enemy Planes,'" 1.

Chapter 4

1. Henrietta Miller to R. Chris Santos, 11 May 1974, quoted in Santos, "Doris 'Dorie' Miller," 12.

2. *New York Times*, 16 December 1941, 1, and 22 December 1941, 1, 4. This report is apparently the basis for the erroneous assumption, perpetuated by numerous historians, that Miller was stationed aboard *Arizona* rather than *West Virginia*.

3. Miller, *Messman Chronicles*, 301.

4. Quoted in ibid., 293.

5. "May Cite Messman, Laborers," *Pittsburgh Courier*, 14 February 1942, 1.

6. Aiken, "Doris Miller and His Navy Cross."

7. "Messman Hero Identified," *Pittsburgh Courier*, 14 March 1942. This is the earliest known use of "Dorie," an apparent typographical error. Some sources have further misspelled the name as "Dore" and "Dorrie." Various writers have attributed "Dorie" to other suggestions, such as a "nickname to shipmates and friends" or the notion that "the Navy thought he should go by the more masculine-sounding Dorie." Aiken, "Doris Miller and His Navy Cross," n.p.

8. Given Miller's eighth-grade education, the effort was doomed to failure; not only did the messman's academic deficiencies disqualify him, but the navy had no intention of training a black man to become a commissioned officer, responding to those who sent in recommendations with a form letter stating that at age twenty-two, Miller was "too old for appointment."

9. Quoted in "I Had to Spank Doris to Make Him Protect Himself," *Pittsburgh Courier*, 14 May 1942, 4.

10. "Editorial," *Pittsburgh Courier*, 14 February 1942, 3; "Mr. Miller and Mr. Lockard," *Pittsburgh Courier*, 21 March 1942, 6.

11. "President May Give Dorie Miller Medal," *Pittsburgh Courier*, 9 May 1942, 6.

12. Peter Collier, *Medal of Honor: Portraits of Valor beyond the Call of Duty* (Sioux City, IA: Artisan, 2003), 156, 183, 184, 189, 206, 210, 213, 239, 248, 252, 258, 270, 272, 277, 285.

13. Ramsey quoted in Levin, "Long War of Doris Miller"; "Movie May Detail Waco Man's Heroism at Pearl Harbor," *Austin American-Statesman*, 14 August 1990, B3.

14. Knox, in civilian life a Republican newspaper publisher and an army officer in World War I, had been appointed secretary of the navy mostly to create the bipartisan image FDR sought. *Washington Times-Herald*, 12 May 1942.

15. White quoted in *Chicago Defender*, 27 December 1941.

16. Du Bois, *Dusk of Dawn*, 127.

17. White quoted in *Chicago Defender*, 27 December 1941; Prattis, "Morale of the Negro in the Armed Services," 355; James G. Thompson, "Should I Sacrifice to Live Half-American?" (letter to editor), *Pittsburgh Courier*, 11 April 1942.

18. Quoted in Suggs, *Black Press in the South*, 407.

19. Golightly, "Negro Higher Education and Democratic Negro Morale," 324.

20. Office of War Information, "Negroes and the War: A Study in Baltimore and Cincinnati, July 21, 1942," Presidential Office Files, Franklin Delano Roosevelt Archives.

21. Quoted in Myrdal, *American Dilemma*, 1006.

22. Du Bois, "Editorial," 164.

23. Thompson, "Should I Sacrifice to Live Half-American?"; Du Bois, "Editorial," 164.

24. Walter White, "What the Negro Thinks of the Army," *Annals of the American Academy of Political and Social Science* 223 (September 1942): 67.

25. "Rogers Interviews a Man Who Was 'Quizzed' by Adolph," *Pittsburgh Courier*, 30 May 1942, 1, 8.

26. Langston Hughes, "Nazi and Dixie Nordics," in DeSaintis, *Langston Hughes and the Chicago Defender*, 79.

27. Hayward "Woody" Farrar, "Identity, Patriotism, and Protest on the Wartime Home Front, 1917–19, 1941–5," in Hornsby, *Companion to African American History*, 372–73.

28. Golightly, "Negro Higher Education and Democratic Negro Morale," 324.

29. Essien-Udom, *Black Nationalism*, 67.

30. "That's Why We're Marching: WWII and the American Folk Song Movement," Smithsonian/Folkways, 1996.

31. Quoted in Washburn, *Question of Sedition*, 83, 84.

32. Nolte, *Strength for the Fight*; Rampersad, *Jackie Robinson*; Tygiel, "Court-Martial of Jackie Robinson"; Haley, *Autobiography of Malcolm X*, 382.

33. Quoted in "I Had to Spank Doris to Make Him Protect Himself," *Pittsburgh Courier*, 14 May 1942, 4.

34. William Henry, interview, quoted in Miller, *Messman Chronicles*, 298.

35. Cansleb, "Nation Pays Tribute to Parent of Naval Hero," 1.

36. Vito Marcantonio to Con[n]ery Miller, 9 March 1942, in Annette T. Rubinstein, ed., *I Vote My Conscience: Debates, Speeches and Writings of Vito Marcantonio, 1935–1950* (New York: Vito Marcantonio Memorial, 1956), 156–57; "Congressman Pays Tribute to Miller," *Pittsburgh Courier*, 21 March 1943.

37. Wendell Willkie, "What Are We Fighting For?" *New York PM*, 6 April

1942; "Willkie Says He'd End Navy Jim Crow," *Afro-American*, 4 April 1942, 1, 2, quoted in Miller, *Messman Chronicles*, 296.

38. Quoted in "Willkie Championed Cause of Negro Americans," *Pittsburgh Courier*, 14 October 1944, 10.

39. Quoted in "Deeds of Joe Louis and Dorie Miller Cited in Address," *Dallas Express*, 28 March 1942, 3.

40. Quoted in Miller, *Messman Chronicles*, 291.

41. "These Men Developed the 'Double V' Idea," *Pittsburgh Courier*, 11 April 1942, 5.

42. Quoted in Miller, *Messman Chronicles*, 291–92.

43. Ibid., 292–93.

44. Quoted in ibid., 293–94.

45. *Pittsburgh Courier*, 21 March 1942, 6.

46. Quoted in *Army and Navy Journal* 79 (16 May 1942): 1018; *Pittsburgh Courier*, 13 March 1942, 1.

47. *Pittsburgh Courier*, 11 May 1942, 3; *Army and Navy Journal* 79 (16 May 1942): 1018.

48. "Honors Due for Waco Parents of Negro War Hero," *Waco Tribune-Herald*, 5 April 1942.

49. Francis Biddle to Franklin D. Roosevelt, 1 May 1942, quoted in Parker, *A Man Called Doris*, 88.

50. Walker to Bard, 13 May 1942, Bard Papers, quoted in Miller, *Messman Chronicles*, 303; Schwartz, "Sinking of the *Liscome Bay*," 8.

51. "Dorie Miller Not in States, Navy Declares," *Pittsburgh Courier*, 23 May 1942, 1.

52. After a distinguished career in the Aleutians and the Pacific, *Indianapolis*, then at Mare Island for major repairs and an overhaul, received orders to proceed to the US air base on Tinian Island, carrying the Uranium-235 for the atomic bomb, "Little Boy," which was to be dropped on Hiroshima. *Indianapolis* departed San Francisco on 16 July 1945, within hours of the Trinity test, and delivered the weapon components to Tinian on 26 July. Then ordered to Leyte, on 30 July 1945 *Indianapolis* was struck on its starboard bow by two torpedoes from the Imperial Japanese Navy submarine *I-58*, sinking within twelve minutes. An estimated 300 men were killed in secondary explosions. An estimated 900 sailors were set adrift in the ocean, where they remained undetected for nearly four days and nights. By the time rescue arrived, all but 317 men had died. This was the greatest single loss of life at sea in the history of the US Navy. Newcomb, *Abandon Ship!*; Stanton, *In Harm's Way*.

53. Quoted in *Pittsburgh Courier*, 23 November 1940; Moore, *Fighting for America*, 33.

Chapter 5

1. "Negro[e]s Not to Blame for Pearl Harbor, Thanks to Navy Jim Crow," *Dallas Express*, 3 January 1941, quoted in Astor, *Right to Fight*, 160.

2. Ibid., 158.

3. Wynn, *Afro-American and the Second World War*, 23.

4. "Conference Findings Section Raps U.S. Military Services," *Newport News Press*, 27 November 1940.

5. Morris J. MacGregor and Bernard C. Nalty, eds., *Blacks in the United States Armed Forces: Basic Documents*, vol. 6, *Blacks in the World War II Naval Establishment* (New York: Rowman & Littlefield, 1977), 22.

6. Quoted in Miller, *Messman Chronicles*, 355.

7. The navy received its first black ensign in June 1942, but not until April 1944 did any sizable number of black officers come on board when twenty-two new ensigns were commissioned—out of a total of 70,000 serving naval officers. Of these men, twelve came from the ranks, and the remaining ten were physicians and dentists. During the war no black naval officer achieved a rank higher than lieutenant. During this period, recruiting for the messman branch continued without interruption, although the men in that rating were soon to be reclassified as stewards. Reddick, "The Negro in the United States Navy," 202–3, 212.

8. Ibid., 208; Murray Florence, ed., *The Negro Handbook* (New York: Wendell Malliet and Company, 1942), 110. See also *New York Age*, 25 April 1942, 6; "Varying Degrees of Opinion Greet New Navy Policy," *Pittsburg Courier*, 18 April 1942, 1; and *Brooklyn Daily Eagle*, 12 April 1942, 35.

9. *Houston Informer*, 25 April 1942.

10. *Philadelphia Tribune*, 18 April 1942.

11. "Courier Campaigns for Return of Dorie," *Pittsburgh Courier*, 25 June 1942, 1.

12. Quoted in Nelson, *Integration of the Negro*, 15–16, 37–38. On 23 February 1944, the Navy Department announced that two antisubmarine vessels would be commissioned and manned with all-black crews, including the ships' twenty-two commissioned officers. In August 1944 the navy assigned black sailors to twenty-five auxiliary ships. These seamen, however, were integrated completely with white crews. Finally, in December 1945, the secretary of the navy issued a directive that "in the administration of naval personnel no differentiation shall be made because of race or color." And at last, on 27 February 1946, the navy opened general service assignments without any restriction. "Effective immediately all restrictions covering governing types of assignments for which Negro naval personnel are eligible are hereby lifted. Henceforth they shall be eligible for all types of assignments in all ratings in all activities and all ships of the naval service. . . . In the utilization of

housing, messing and other facilities, no special or unusual provisions will be made for the accommodation of Negro[e]s." President's Committee on Equality of Treatment and Opportunity in the Armed Services, *Freedom to Serve*, 6, 17–30.

13. "Mr. Knox Hasn't Said Enough, This Paper Still Believes in a Navy without Barriers," *Pittsburgh Courier*, 18 April 1942, 1.

14. Not until 13 April 1945 did the navy remove all restrictions on numbers and types of vessels to which black personnel could be assigned. During the summer of 1945 the all-black Great Lakes Camp Robert Smalls was phased out and all boot training was integrated. Black recruits were assigned to the same companies, barracks, and messes as whites.

15. "Mr. Knox Hasn't Said Enough," *Pittsburgh Courier*, 18 April 1942, 1.

16. "Two-Race Navy Is Denounced by New York Racial Club," *Pittsburgh Courier*, 25 April 1942, 2.

17. "Varying Degrees of Opinion Greet New Naval Policy," *Pittsburgh Courier*, 18 April 1942, 1.

18. "We Are Americans, Too!" *Pittsburgh Courier*, 13 December 1941, 1; *Pittsburgh Courier*, 14 February 1942; Buni, *Robert L. Vann*; Finkle, *Forum for Protest*.

19. Brant, *Harlem and War*; "We Are Americans, Too!" *Pittsburgh Courier*, 13 December 1941), 1. In 1942 other black newspapers, including the *Los Angeles Sentinel*, the *Washington Tribune*, the *Columbus* (Ohio) *Challenger*, the *Aiken* (South Carolina) *Journal*, the *Rochester* (New York) *Voice*, the Interracial News Service, and a periodical of the Federal Council of Churches also became advocates for the Double V campaign.

20. "We Are Americans, Too!" *Pittsburgh Courier*, 14 December 1941, 1; *Pittsburgh Courier*, 14 February 1942; Buni, *Robert L. Vann*; Finkle, *Forum for Protest*.

21. Miller quoted in *Pittsburgh Courier*, 26 September 1942, 5.

22. Takaki, *Double Victory*.

23. Kersten, "African Americans and World War II," 13–14.

24. Ibid.; Benjamin F. McLaurin, interview by William Ingersoll, 1960, Columbia Center for Oral History, New York, NY; Anderson, *A. Phillip Randolph*.

25. This did not occur, however, until 1944 on the watch of Knox's replacement, James Forrestal. The destroyer escort *Mason* and the submarine chaser *PC-1264* were commanded by white officers but with all-black crews. Both proved effective at protecting Allied convoys from German submarines in the North Atlantic, convincing the navy that blacks could handle at-sea combat jobs. Kelly, *Proudly We Served*; Blackford, *On Board the USS* Mason.

26. Nalty, *Strength for the Fight*; Sitwell, *Golden Thirteen*.

27. "Dorie Miller, Hero at Pearl Harbor, Speaks," *Dallas Express*, 23 January 1943, 1.

28. Quoted in ibid.

29. Kinloch, "Back from Kiska," 1.

Chapter 6

1. "Doris Miller's Medal Pinned," *Waco Times-Herald*, 28 May 1942; "Courier Campaigns for Return of Dorie," *Pittsburgh Courier*, 25 June 1942, 1; Schuyler, "The World Today," 1.

2. "Courier Campaigns for Return of Dorie," *Pittsburgh Courier*, 25 June 1942, 1.

3. Ibid.; "Willkie Pledges Aid in Fight to Return Dorie," *Pittsburgh Courier*, 11 July 1942, 4.

4. Miller quoted in *Pittsburgh Courier*, 26 September 1942, 4.

5. "A Hero Returns; A Medal He Wears," *Pittsburgh Courier*, 19 December 1942, 1. In 1942 the Navy Distinguished Service Medal came before the Navy Cross in order of precedence. Authority to award the medal was ordinarily delegated to the secretary of the navy and commanding officers, so the president's personally issuing the award in Miller's case was something of a rarity.

6. Ibid.; "Navy Pacific Hero Home on Furlough," *Pittsburgh Courier*, 2 January 1943; "Dorie Miller Thrills Naval Graduating Class with Talk," *Pittsburgh Courier*, 16 January 1943.

7. Quoted in Joseph, "'I Downed Four Enemy Planes,'" 1.

8. "Presentation to Dorie Miller," *Pittsburgh Courier*, 2 January 1943, 19.

9. Adams, "From Squirrels to Bombers," 10A.

10. "Christmas 1942," typescript transcription of unidentified newspaper article, in possession of authors; "Son Died in Vain, Says Dorie Miller's Father," *Baltimore Afro-American*, 15 December 1945, 1, 19.

11. Johnson, "Honoring Dorie Miller."

12. *Waco Messenger*, 22 January 1943, 2; Radford, *African-American Heritage in Waco*, 257.

13. "No Time to Think, Says Negro Who Won Navy Cross," *Dallas Morning News*, 20 January 1943, 6.

14. "Dinner to Honor Texas Negro Who Won Navy Cross," *Dallas Morning News*, 2 January 1943, 7; "No Time to Think, Says Negro Who Won Navy Cross," *Dallas Morning News*, 20 January 1943, 6; "Negro Tells Students of Pearl Harbor Battle," *Dallas Morning News*, 21 January 1943, 6. *Waco Messenger* quoted in Radford, *African-American Heritage in Waco*, 257.

15. Quoted in Smith, "Valor at Sunrise," A1.

16. Quoted in ibid., A12.

17. Quoted in ibid.

18. Camp Robert Smalls was named in honor of an enslaved African American who, on 13 May 1862, commandeered the Confederate transport *Planter* and sailed it to freedom under the guns of the federal ships then blockading Charleston, South Carolina. This act of daring is said to have influenced President Abraham Lincoln in his decision to arm black men in the Union cause. Davis, "The Negro in the United States Navy, Marine Corps and Coast Guard," 346–47.

19. Armstrong quoted in Anderson, *Education of Blacks in the South*, 33–47, 328.

20. Nelson, *Integration of the Negro*, 27–33.

21. Shirley Moody-Turner, *Black Folklore and the Politics of Racial Representation* (Jackson: University Press of Mississippi, 2013), 59.

22. "97 Bluejackets Finish Great Lakes Training," *Pittsburgh Courier*, 30 January 1943, 24.

23. Quoted in "First Bluejackets Finish; Addressed by Doris Miller," *Dallas Express*, 30 January 1943, 1.

24. Quoted in Joseph, "'I Downed Four Enemy Planes,'" 1.

25. Quoted in "Dorie Miller Talks to Camp Smalls Grads," *Baltimore Afro-American*, 16 January 1943, 3; "First Bluejackets Finish; Addressed by Doris Miller," 1.

26. C. Robert Jenkins, interview, 3 October 1999, quoted in Miller, *Messman Chronicles*, 306.

27. Johns, "Dorie Miller Is Modest," 1, 2.

28. Quoted in Joseph, "'I Downed Four Enemy Planes,'" 1.

29. "I Had to Spank Doris to Make Him Protect Himself," *Pittsburgh Courier*, 14 May 1942, 4; "Mrs. Miller Is Guest Speaker on 'Wings' Program over KTRH," *Dallas Express*, 16 May 1942, 1.

30. He was not, as he has often been called, a "ship's cook" and still belonged to the messman branch, a name not officially changed to the steward branch until later in 1943.

31. USS *Liscome Bay* (CVE-56) had been commissioned on 7 August 1943.

32. Although the ship's muster rolls do not identify sailors by race, one can assume, based on established navy policies of the day—with the apparent exception of Steward's Mate 1st Class Irineo Almazan of Salinas, California—that they were exclusively black.

33. Francis Daily, interview, 17 July 2001 and 6 January 2002, quoted in Noles, *Twenty-Three Minutes to Eternity*, 29.

34. Kaderlik, "Haynes Survived Sinking of USS *Liscome Bay*," n.p.

35. Among the dead was Admiral Mullinnix, who had graduated first in the naval academy class of 1916 and became one of the navy's first "air admirals," and Capt. Irving D. Wiltsie, the ship's captain. Capt. John G. Crommelin Jr.,

Mullinnix's chief of staff, was the senior officer to survive the sinking. Later in his career Crommelin, a decorated naval aviator, sparked the so-called "Revolt of the Admirals," which helped save the role of naval aviation. Noles, *Twenty-Three Minutes to Eternity*; Burns, "USS *Liscome Bay* Survivors."

Chapter 7

1. "Negro Hero Reported Lost in Pacific Action," *Dallas Morning News*, 9 December 1943, 4. A memorial service at Waco's Second Baptist Church on 30 April 1944 received national attention.

2. When asked whether things were better because of his son's sacrifice, without hesitating Miller responded with a resolute *No.* "If I could have my ruther's, I'd rather have my son back!" The elder Miller did, however, express satisfaction that since his son's heroic action at Pearl Harbor the navy had dropped its color bars and was allowing black seamen to get training in gunnery. "Son Died in Vain, Says Dorie Miller's Father," *Baltimore Afro-American*, December 15, 1945, 1, 19.

3. Quoted in Smith, "Valor at Sunrise," A12.

4. Prattis, "Morale of the Negro in the Armed Services," 362; Davis, *Story of the First Pioneer Infantry.*

5. James, *Double V*, 170.

6. Buni, *Robert L. Vann.*

7. In 1943 mess attendants became steward's mates, and in 1944 cooks and stewards were authorized to wear petty officer–style rating insignia, although they did not officially receive petty officer status until 1 January 1950. In addition, it announced in June 1950 that stewards would have the privilege, if qualified, of transferring to other ratings. Even then, steward ratings continued to carry the stigma of servitude and second-class status, a stigma that was only reinforced when, later in the 1950s, the navy resumed enlistment of men from the Republic of the Philippines exclusively for steward duty. Even so, as late as February 1950 approximately 57 percent of the 14,000 black enlisted men in the US Navy were still in the steward's branch. In 1974 the rating of steward became amalgamated with that of commissary men. President's Committee on Equality of Treatment and Opportunity in the Armed Services, *Freedom to Serve*, 6, 28.

8. "Remembering Pearl Harbor!" *Pittsburg Courier*, 8 December 1956; see also "Navy Bias Shaken by Mess Hero," *Pittsburgh Courier*, 3 September 1960. Miller, *Messman Chronicles*, 285; Goodwin, *No Ordinary Time*, 329.

9. *Pittsburg Courier*, 8 December 1956; "Navy Bias Shaken by Mess Hero," 3 September 1960.

10. Roucek, "Hopes of Intercultural Education"; Connery Miller quoted in Ceplair, *The Marxist and the Movies*, 79.

11. Quoted in Calamur, "Muhammad Ali and Vietnam," n.p. For interesting commentary on this famous quotation, see Lemert, *Muhammad Ali*, and Westheider, *African American Experience in Vietnam*.

12. Kinloch, "Back from Kiska," 1.

13. Hughes, *Collected Poems*, 191.

14. Miller, *Messman Chronicles*, 286; Miller quoted in Kinloch, "Back from Kiska," 1.

15. Takaki, *Double Victory*, 7.

16. *Pittsburgh Courier*, 26 September 1942, 5.

17. Klinkner, *Unsteady March*, 3–4.

18. Lanning, *African-American Soldier*, 201.

19. Sitwell, *Golden Thirteen*, 193.

20. Dunn, *On Board the USS* Mason.

21. Parker and Klinkner quoted in Tilove, "Six Decades after WWII's End," n.p. For Klinkner's commentary on Doris Miller, see his *Unsteady March*, 161–62, 201.

22. Reddick, "The Negro in the United States Navy," 205.

23. "A Cross to Messman Miller," *New York Times*, 13 May 1942, 18. Lanning, *African American Soldier*.

24. Kinloch, "Back from Kiska," 1.

25. Quoted in ibid.

26. Quoted in Lou Cannon, *Governor Reagan: His Rise to Power* (New York: Public Affairs, 2003), 410–11; Edmund Morris, *Dutch: A Memoir of Ronald Reagan* (New York: Random House, 1999), 397–98; Perlstein, *Invisible Bridge*, 552.

27. Langston Hughes, "December 7, 1941," in *The Collected Works of Langston Hughes*, vol. 2, *The Poems, 1941–1950*, edited by Arnold Rampersad (Columbia: University of Missouri Press, 2001), 99.

28. White quoted in Marjorie E. Greene, "Josh White Starts Them Listening," *Opportunity: Journal of Negro Life* 22, no. 3 (1944): 113; Elijah Wald, *Josh White: Society Blues* (New York: Routledge, 2002), 106–8.

29. Gwendolyn Brooks, "Negro Hero: To Suggest Dorie Miller," in Lehman and Brehm, *Oxford Book of American Poetry*, 625–26.

30. By 1990, the Doris Miller award had been renamed the American Heritage and Freedom Award. Fountain, "Black Navy Captain Is Honored," 84.

31. Jordan quoted in Carter, "U.S.S. Doris Miller Goes to Sea after Commissioning Ceremony." See also "Ship Honoring Dorie Miller Commissioned," *Pittsburgh Courier*, 21 July 1973. In addition to the Navy Cross, Miller was awarded the Purple Heart Medal; the American Defense Service Medal, Fleet Clasp; the Asiatic-Pacific Campaign Medal; and the World War II Victory Medal. The original medals were destroyed when Henrietta Miller's home at 1213 Southey Street burned in 1957, but the navy replaced them in a ceremony

held at East Waco's Doris Miller YMCA. Miller, *Doris Miller*, 70–71; Chester, "'Negroes' Number One Hero,'" 31–61; Radford, *African-American Heritage in Waco*, 254. Dr. Radford, who died in 1987, is buried in Waco's Doris Miller Memorial Park near the graves of Henrietta and Connery Miller.

32. Quoted in Walton, "Mark of Heroism."

33. One of the first African Americans to sing on Broadway, Bledsoe is perhaps best known for having performed as Joe in the 1927 production of *Show Boat*, popularizing Jerome Kern and Oscar Hammerstein's iconic song "Old Man River."

34. "Waco VA Center Renamed to Honor World War II Hero," *Waco Tribune-Herald*, 20 February 2015, 1A, 2A, and 6A; school principal quoted in Chester, "'Negroes' Number One Hero,'" 47.

35. "Doris Miller: Hospital's Renaming Invites Us All to Ponder America's Past, Potential," *Waco Tribune-Herald*, 14 December 1994.

36. "Dedicate Unbiased N.Y. Project," *Chicago Defender*, 26 December 1953.

37. Fowler quoted in Fountain, "Black Navy Captain Is Honored," and in Mel Reynolds, "Tribute to Rev. Elmer L. Fowler [by] Hon. Mel Reynolds of Illinois, House of Representatives, Monday May 23, 1994," *Congressional Record*, 103rd Cong., 2nd Sess., vol. 140, no. 65 (Washington: Government Printing Office, 1994), 11482–83.

38. Quoted in "Entire Navy Awarded Dorie Miller Trophy," *Baltimore Afro-American*, 14 October 1950, 1, 2.

39. According to the Hollywood Marxist's biographer, Paul Jarrico rigged the competition so that the theater, which, significantly, played to integrated audiences, was named for Miller. Ceplair, *The Marxist and the Movies*, 78–79; "Son Died in Vain, Says Dorie Miller's Father," *Baltimore Afro-American*, 15 December 1945, 1, 19.

40. These were Adm. Arleigh A. Burke, who was one of the top destroyer squadron commanders of World War II, and who, after the war, played a major role in modernizing the navy and guiding its response to the Cold War; Vice Adm. William S. Sims, who served as commander of US naval forces in European waters during World War I; and Lt. Cmdr. John McCloy, one of the few men to earn two Medals of Honor for separate acts of heroism.

41. Kinloch, "Back from Kiska," 1.

42. Miller, *Doris Miller*, 74.

43. "New 20th Century-Fox Film to Touch Exploits of Dorie Miller," *Pittsburgh Courier*, 12 September 1942; Cripps, *Making Movies Black*, 58, 76, 110; Buckley, *American Patriots*, 282.

44. *Times* review quoted in Cagle, "Cinema: Pearl Harbor's Top Gun," 69.

45. James E. Nierle to Marsha Rose Joyner, 27 March 2012, quoted in Joyner, "The United States Navy Refuses to Acknowledge Its Racist Past."

46. Ross L. Fowler to William J. Clinton, 30 March 1999, Emerson Emory Papers, AR 466, box 1, folder 10, Special Collections, University of Texas at Arlington Libraries. According to the US Army's official blog, "although not required by law or military regulation, service members are encouraged to salute Medal of Honor recipients as a gesture of respect and courtesy regardless of rank or status and, if the recipients are wearing the medal, whether or not they are in uniform. This is the only instance where a Soldier will receive a salute from members of a higher rank." Brittany Brown, "The Medal of Honor: Eight Surprising Facts," 15 March 2013, *Army Live* (blog), http://armylive.dod live.mil/index.php/2013/03/the-medal-of-honor-eight-surprising-facts.

47. Notation in Emerson's hand on the Bureau of Naval Personnel's reply to Emerson's inquiry as to Miller's service. Emerson Emory Papers, box 10, folder 4, Special Collections, University of Texas at Arlington Libraries.

48. Johnson, "Honoring Dorie Miller"; John D. Dingell to Ross L. Fowler, 9 July 1996, Special Collections, University of Texas at Arlington Libraries.

49. Quoted in Kelly Watson, "Eligibility for Some Awards Extended to Veterans," *Shift Colors* 41, no. 2 (summer 1996): 12.

50. Repko, "Dallas Representative Eddie Bernice Johnson, Others Still Seek Medal of Honor for Pearl Harbor Hero 'Dorie' Miller."

51. "7 Black World War II Vets Awarded Medal of Honor," *USA Today*, 14 January 1997.

52. Of the seven recipients, only one, Vernon Baker, a career army officer, was still living. Bennett, "Medals of Honor Awarded at Last to Black World War II Soldiers."

53. Nierle to Joyner, quoted in Joyner, "The United States Navy Refuses to Acknowledge Its Racist Past."

54. Johnson quoted in Tilove, "Six Decades after WWII's End." See also Johnson, "Honoring Dorie Miller"; Repko, "Dallas Rep. Eddie Bernice Johnson, Others Still Seek Medal of Honor for Pearl Harbor Hero 'Dorie' Miller"; Rudner, "Dorie Miller's Fans Keep Fighting to Honor Black Sailor's Pearl Harbor Heroism."

55. The first biography of Miller, *Doris Miller: Pearl Harbor Hero*, is the work of his niece, Vickie Gail Miller, of Midland, Texas.

56. Repko, "Dallas Representative Eddie Bernice Johnson, Others Still Seek Medal of Honor for Pearl Harbor Hero 'Dorie' Miller." President Obama did rectify at least one such injustice, when, at a White House ceremony in March 2014, he awarded the Medal of Honor to twenty-four veterans of World War II and the Korean and Vietnam wars—most of them Hispanic—who had been unjustly denied the honor because of their race, religion, or ethnicity. All but three received the award posthumously. One of those men was Santiago Jesus Erevia, a native of Corpus Christi, Texas, who, before joining the

101st Airborne Division, had picked cotton as a day laborer in the Rio Grande Valley. On 21 May 1969, near Tam Kỳ, a coastal town south of Da Nang in South Vietnam, he and a group of wounded Americans under his care came under intense fire from an entrenched enemy unit. Sergeant Erevia, according to the award's citation, "fought his way to the final bunker, running and firing both M-16 rifles simultaneously, and killed the fortification's defenders with point-blank fire." Langer, "Santiago Erevia."

57. Other people of color, women, and gays have been similarly honored. "In the Navy, per traditional ship-naming convention," said Secretary of the Navy Ray Mabus, "our guided missile destroyers are named after heroes." In 2016 Secretary Mabus announced the naming of a new Arleigh Burke–class guided missile destroyers in honor of black Marine Corps lieutenant general Frank E. Petersen Jr., a highly decorated pilot, and Lenah H. Sutcliffe Higbee, who served as superintendent of the Navy Nurse Corps during World War I and was the only living woman to receive the Navy Cross. Other ships in the class are named for women's rights activist Lucy Stone and abolitionist Sojourner Truth.

The navy also honored slain gay rights activist and former San Francisco supervisor Harvey Milk by naming a Military Sealift Command fleet oiler after him. The USNS *Harvey Milk* is a John Lewis–class vessel, a series of vessels named for civil rights icons. Milk served as a lieutenant in the navy during the Korean War, and according to his nephew, Stuart Milk, "We have just reached the point recently where LGBT people can serve openly in the military, and what better message can there be of that than this ship?"

"I've spoken with sailors and Marines about being deployed, about what sustains them throughout deployments, and about what drives them to be so good at what they do," Secretary Mabus said. "And that spirit is not about gender, race or who you love; it's about selflessness and character." "Navy Secretary Names Destroyer after Female Navy Cross Recipient," n.p.

58. Jordan quoted in Carter, "U.S.S. Dorie Miller Goes to Sea after Commissioning Ceremony," and in Henderson, "Ship Named for Waco Hero."

59. "Navy Transfers Ship Named for Wacoan," *Waco Tribune-Herald*, 24 January 1984; Serdar Akinsel to Emerson Emory, 6 March 2001, Emerson Emory Papers, box 10, folder 4, Special Collections, University of Texas at Arlington Libraries.

60. "Dining Hall Named for Doris Miller," *Waco News-Tribune*, 4 June 1970.

61. "Waco War Hero Honored Tuesday," *Waco Citizen*, 9 December 1971.

62. Quoted in "Waco Pearl Harbor Hero Honored with Dedication of the Navy Quarters," *Waco News-Tribune*, 8 December 1971.

63. Quoted in "Navy Honors Black Pearl Harbor Hero," 46–47; Sherwood, *Black Sailor, White Navy*, 41–42.

64. Reddick, "The Negro in the United States Navy," 217; *Navy Department Bulletin*, 28, 28 February 1946; Forestall quoted in Nalty, *Strength for the Fight*, 196–97.

65. Quoted in Smith, "Austin Service Celebrates Doris Miller," 3B.

66. Reddick, "The Negro in the United States Navy," 217–19; Zumwalt quoted in "Keelhauling the United States Navy," *Time*, 27 November 1972, 20–21.

67. Sherwood, *Black Sailor, White Navy*; Martin Luther King Jr., "Beyond Vietnam," speech delivered at Riverside Church, New York, 4 April 1967, in Clayborne Carson et al., eds., *Eyes on the Prize: America's Civil Rights Years; A Reader and Guide* (New York: Penguin, 1987), 201.

68. Stokely Carmichael, "Speech at Garfield High School, Seattle, Washington," 19 April 1967, http://www.aavw.org/special_features/speeches_speech _carmichael01.html.

69. Perry, "Navy Hero's Mother Bitter," 45.

70. Miller, *Messman Chronicles*, 316.

71. Ibid.

Bibliography

Archival Material

Bard Papers. US Department of the Navy. Records of the Office of the Assistant Secretary of the Navy (Ralph Bard), Correspondence Relating to Discrimination in the Navy 1941–44, AO-172, RG 80, NARA, Washington, DC.

Emerson Emory Papers. Special Collections, University of Texas at Arlington Libraries, Arlington, TX.

Franklin Delano Roosevelt Archives. FDR Presidential Library and Museum, Hyde Park, NY.

Lamar Richard Papers. Eisenhower Center for American Studies, University of New Orleans, New Orleans, LA.

Thomas E. Turner Sr. Papers. Texas Collection, Baylor University, Waco, TX.

Books

Albright, Alex. *Forgotten First: B-1 and the Integration of the Modern Navy.* Fountain, NC: R. A. Fountain, 2013.

Altoff, Gerald T. *Amongst My Best Men: African Americans and the War of 1812.* Put-in-Bay, OH: Perry Group, 1996.

Anderson, James D. *The Education of Blacks in the South, 1860–1935.* Chapel Hill: University of North Carolina Press, 1988.

Anderson, Jervis. *A. Phillip Randolph: A Biographical Portrait.* Berkeley: University of California Press, 1973.

Astor, Gerald. *The Right to Fight: A History of African Americans in the Military.* Novato, CA: Presidio Press, 1998.

Barnes, Marian E. *Black Texans: They Overcame.* Austin, TX: Eakin Press, 1996.

Bennett, Michael J. *Union Jacks: Yankee Sailors in the Civil War.* Chapel Hill: University of North Carolina Press, 2004.

Bernstein, Patricia. *The First Waco Horror: The Lynching of Jesse Washington and the Rise of the NAACP.* College Station: Texas A&M University Press, 2005.

Blackford, Mansel G., ed. *On Board the USS* Mason: *The World War II Diary of James A. Dunn.* Columbus: Ohio State University Press, 1996.

Bolster, W. Jeffery. *Black Jacks: African American Seamen in the Age of Sail.* Cambridge, MA: Harvard University Press, 1997.

Bracken, Sharon, ed. *Historic McLennan County: An Illustrated History.* San Antonio, TX: Historical Publishing Network, 2011.

Brands, H. W. *The General vs. the President: MacArthur and Truman at the Brink of Nuclear War.* New York, NY: Doubleday, 2016.

Brant, Nat. *Harlem at War: The Black Experience in World War II.* Secaucus, NY: Syracuse University Press, 1996.

Buchanan, A. Russell. *Black Americans in World War II.* Santa Barbara, CA: Clio Books, 1997.

Buckley, Gail. *American Patriots: The Story of Blacks in the Military from the Revolution to Desert Storm.* New York: Random House, 2001.

Buni, Andrew. *Robert L. Vann of the* Pittsburgh Courier: *Politics and Black Journalism.* Pittsburgh: University of Pittsburgh Press, 1974.

Carver, Charles. *Brann and the Iconoclast.* Austin: University of Texas Press, 1957.

Ceplair, Larry. *The Marxist and the Movies: A Biography of Paul Jarrico.* Lexington: University of Kentucky Press, 2007.

Cotham, Edward Terrel, ed. *The Southern Journey of a Civil War Marine: The Illustrated Note-book of Henry O. Gusley.* Austin: University of Texas Press, 2006.

Cripps, Thomas. *Making the Movies Black: The Hollywood Message Movie from World War I to the Civil Rights Era.* New York: Oxford University Press, 1993.

Cutler, Thomas J. *A Sailor's History of the U.S. Navy.* Annapolis, MD: Naval Institute Press, 2005.

Dalfiume, Richard M. *Desegregation of the US Armed Forces: Fighting on Two Fronts, 1939–1953.* Columbia: University of Missouri Press, 1969.

David, Jay, and Elaine Crane. *The Black Soldier from the American Revolution to Vietnam.* New York: William Morrow and Co., 1971.

Davis, Chester W. *The Story of the First Pioneer Infantry, U.S.A.* Utica, NY: Kirkland Press, 1919.

DeSaintis, Christopher C., ed. *Langston Hughes and the Chicago Defender: Essays on Race, Politics, and Culture, 1942–62.* Urbana: University of Illinois Press, 1995.

Douglass, Frederick. *Life and Times of Frederick Douglass.* Hartford, CT: Park Publishing Co., 1881.

Du Bois, W. E. B. *Dusk of Dawn: An Essay toward an Autobiography of a Race Concept.* New York: Oxford University Press, 2007.

Essien-Udom, Essien Udosen. *Black Nationalism: A Search for Identity in America.* Chicago: University of Chicago Press, 1962.

Finkle, Lee H. *Forum for Protest: The Black Press during World War II*. East Rutherford, NJ: Fairleigh Dickinson University Press, 1975.

Fletcher, Marvin. *The Negro Soldier in the United States Army, 1891–1970*. Columbia: University of Missouri Press, 1974.

Foner, Jack. *Blacks and the Military in American History*. New York: Prager, 1974.

Franklin, John Hope. *From Slavery to Freedom: A History of Negro Americans*, 3rd ed. New York: Alfred A. Knopf, 1969.

Glasrud, Bruce A., ed. *Anti-Black Violence in Twentieth-Century Texas*. College Station: Texas A&M University Press, 2015.

Goodwin, Doris Kearns. *No Ordinary Time: Franklin and Eleanor Roosevelt; The Home Front in World War II*. New York: Simon and Schuster, 1995.

Haley, Alex, ed. *The Autobiography of Malcolm X*. New York: Grove Press, 1966.

Harrod, Frederick S. *Manning the New Navy: The Development of a Modern Naval Enlisted Force, 1899–1940*. Westport, CT: Greenwood Press, 1978.

Haynes, Richard F. *The Awesome Power: Harry S. Truman as Commander in Chief*. Baton Rouge: Louisiana State University Press, 1978.

Hope, Richard O. *Racial Strife in the Military: Toward the Elimination of Discrimination*. New York: Praeger, 1979.

Hornsby, Alton, Jr., ed. *Companion to African American History*. Malden, MA: Blackwell Publishing, 2005.

Howarth, Stephen. *To Shining Sea: A History of the United States Navy, 1775–1991*. New York: Random House, 1991.

Hughes, Langston. *The Collected Poems of Langston Hughes*. New York: Alfred A. Knopf, 1994.

James, Rawn, Jr. *The Double V: How Wars, Protest, and Harry Truman Desegregated America's Military*. New York: Bloomsbury Press, 2013.

Karig, Walter. *Battle Report: Pearl Harbor to Coral Sea*. New York: Farrar & Rinehart, 1944.

Kilpatrick, James Jackson. *The Southern Case for School Segregation*. New York: Crowell-Collier Press, 1962.

Kelly, Mary Pat. *Proudly We Served: The Men of the USS* Mason. Annapolis, MD: U.S. Naval Institute Press, 1995.

Klinkner, Philip A. *The Unsteady March: The Rise and Decline of Racial Equality in America*. New Haven, CT: Yale University Press, 1994.

Kryder, Daniel. *Divided Arsenal: Race and the American State during World War II*. New York: Cambridge University Press, 2000.

Langley, Harold D. *Social Reform in the United States Navy, 1798 through 1862*. Chicago: University of Illinois Press, 1967.

Lanning, Michael Lee. *The African-American Soldier: From Crispus Attucks to Colin Powell*. Secaucus, NJ: Birch Lane Press, 1977.

Lee, James Ward, ed. *1941: Texas Goes to War*. Denton: University of North Texas Press, 1991.

Lehman, David, and John Brehm, eds. *The Oxford Book of American Poetry*. New York: Oxford University Press, 2006.

Lemert, Charles. *Muhammad Ali: Trickster in the Culture of Irony*. New York: Polity, 2003.

Lord, Walter. *Day of Infamy*. New York: Henry Holt, 1957.

MacGregor, Morris J. *Integration of the Armed Forces, 1949–1965*. Washington, DC: Center for Military History, 1989.

McGuire, Phillip. *Taps for a Jim Crow Army*. Lexington: University Press of Kentucky, 1993.

Mackenzie, Alexander Slidell. *The Life of Commodore Oliver Hazard Perry*. 2 vols. New York: Harper and Brothers, 1840.

McMillen, Neil R., ed. *Remaking Dixie: The Impact of World War II on the American South*. Jackson: University Press of Mississippi, 1997.

Miller, Richard E. *The Messman Chronicles: African Americans in the U.S. Navy, 1932–1943*. Annapolis, MD: Naval Institute Press, 2004.

Miller, Vickie Gail. *Doris Miller: A Silent Medal of Honor Winner*. Austin, TX: Eakin Press, 1997.

Moore, Christopher Paul. *Fighting for America: Black Soldiers-the Unsung Heroes of World War II*. New York: Random House, 2005.

Morehouse, Maggi M. *Fighting in the Jim Crow Army: Black Men and Women Remember World War II*. Lanham, MD: Roman and Littlefield, 2000.

Motley, Mary P. *The Invisible Soldier: The Experience of the Black Soldier, World War II*. Detroit, MI: Wayne State University Press, 1975.

Myrdal, Gunner. *American Dilemma*. New York: Harper and Brothers, 1944.

Nalty, Bernard C. *Long Passage to Korea: Black Sailors and the Integration of the U.S. Navy*. Washington, DC: Naval Historical Center, 2003.

———. *Strength for the Fight: A History of Black Americans in the Military*. New York: Free Press, 1986.

Nelson, Craig. *Pearl Harbor: From Infamy to Greatness*. New York: Scribner, 2016.

Nelson, Dennis D. *The Integration of the Negro into the United States Navy, 1776–1947*. 1948. Reprint, New York: Farrar, Straus & Young, 1951.

Newcomb, Richard F. *Abandon Ship!: The Saga of the U.S.S.* Indianapolis, *the Navy's Greatest Sea Disaster*. New York: Harper, 2000.

Noles, James L., Jr. *Twenty-Three Minutes to Eternity: The Final Voyage of the Escort Carrier USS* Liscome Bay. Tuscaloosa: University of Alabama Press, 2004.

Nolte, Bernard. *Strength for the Fight: A History of Black Americans in the Military*. New York: Free Press, 1986.

O'Neal, Bill. *Doris Miller: Hero of Pearl Harbor*. Waco, TX: Eakin Press, 2007.

Parker, Juliete. *A Man Named Doris*. Maitland, FL: Xulon Press, 2003.

Perlstein, Rick. *The Invisible Bridge: The Fall of Nixon and the Rise of Reagan*. New York: Simon and Schuster, 2014.

Potter, Lou, William Miles, and Nina Rosenblum. *Fighting on Two Fronts in World War II*. New York: Harcourt Brace Jovanovich, 1992.

Prange, Gordon W. *At Dawn We Slept: The Untold Story of Pearl Harbor*. New York: McGraw Hill, 1981.

Radford, Garry H., Sr. *African-American Heritage in Waco, Texas*. Austin, TX: Eakin Press, 2000.

Rampersad, Arnold. *Jackie Robinson: A Biography*. New York: Alfred A. Knopf, 1997.

Richardson, Benjamin. *Great American Negroes*. New York: Thomas Y. Crowell, 1956.

Ringle, Dennis J. *Life in Mr. Lincoln's Navy*. Annapolis, MD: Naval Institute Press, 1998.

Selfridge, Thomas O. *What Finer Tradition: The Memoirs of Thomas O. Selfridge, Jr., Rear Admiral, USN*. Columbia: University of South Carolina Press, 1987.

Shaffer, Donald R. *After the Glory: The Struggles of Black Civil War Veterans*. Topeka: University Press of Kansas, 2004.

Sherwood, John Darrell. *Black Sailor, White Navy: Racial Unrest in the Fleet during the Vietnam War Era*. New York: New York University Press, 2007.

Silvera, John D. *The Negro in World War II*. 1946. Reprint, New York: Arno Press; 1969.

Sitton, Thad, and Dan K. Utley. *From Can See to Can't: Texas Cotton Farmers on the Southern Prairies*. Austin: University of Texas Press, 1997.

Sitwell, Paul, ed. *The Golden Thirteen: Recollections of the First Black Naval Officers*. Annapolis, MD: Naval Institute Press, 2003.

Smith, Myron J., Jr. *The Mountain State Battleship: USS* West Virginia. Richwood: West Virginia Press Club, 1981.

Stanton, Doug. *In Harm's Way: The Sinking of the U.S.S.* Indianapolis *and the Extraordinary Story of Its Survivors*. New York: Owl Books, 2003.

Suggs, Henry Lewis. *The Black Press in the South*. New York: Praeger, 1983.

Takaki, Ronald. *Double Victory: A Multicultural History of America in World War II*. New York: Back Bay Books, 2000.

Washburn, Patrick S. *The African American Newspaper: Voice of Freedom*. Evanston, IL: Northwestern University Press, 2006.

———. *A Question of Sedition: The Federal Government's Investigation of the Black Press during World War II*. New York: Oxford University Press, 1986.

Westheider, James E. *The African American Experience in Vietnam: Brothers in Arms*. New York: Rowman and Littlefield, 2007.

Williams, Juan. *Eyes on the Prize: America's Civil Rights Years, 1954–1965.* New York: Viking Penguin, 1987.

Wynn, Neil A. *The Afro-American and the Second World War.* New York: Holmes and Meier Publishers, 1976.

Journal Articles and Scholarly Essays

Armstead, Ron E. "Veterans in the Fight for Equal Rights: From the Civil War to Today." *Trotter Review* 18, no. 1 (2009): 92–105.

Bailey, Beth, and David Farber. "The 'Double V' Campaign in World War II Hawaii: African Americans, Racial Ideology, and Federal Power." *Journal of Social History* 26, no. 4 (summer 1993): 817–43.

Celardo, John. "Shifting Seas: Racial Integration in the United States Navy, 1941–1945." *Prologue* 23, no. 3 (fall 1991): 230–35.

Chester, Robert K. "'Negroes' Number One Hero': Doris Miller, Pearl Harbor, and Retroactive Multiculturalism in World War II Remembrance." *American Quarterly* 65, no. 1 (March 2013): 31–61.

Davis, John W. "The Negro in the United States Navy, Marine Corps and Coast Guard." *Journal of Negro Education* 12 (summer 1943): 345–49.

Duty, Tony. "Waco at the Turn of the Century." *Waco Heritage and History* 3, no. 2 (summer 1972): 1–18.

Golightly, Cornelius L. "Negro Higher Education and Democratic Negro Morale." *Journal of Negro Education* 11 (July 1942): 322–28.

J.J.D.B. "The Time for the Offensive Is Here." *Elementary English Review* 21 (March 1944): 114–15.

Jones, Mark. "Doris Miller: First American Hero of World War II." *Waco Magazine of Heritage and History* 14 (spring 1984): 41–53.

Kersten, Andrew E. "African Americans and World War II." *OAH Magazine of History* 16 (spring 2002): 13–17.

"Negroes in the Navy." Appendix A. *Proceedings of the Massachusetts Historical Society* 6 (1863): 239–42.

Perry, Earnest L., Jr. "It's Time to Force a Change . . ." *Journalism History* 28, no. 2 (summer 2002): 85–95.

Prattis, P. L. "The Morale of the Negro in the Armed Services of the United States." *Journal of Negro Education* 12 (summer 1943): 355–63.

Reddick, L. D. "The Negro in the United States Navy during World War II." *Journal of Negro History* 32 (April 1947): 201–19.

Roucek, Joseph S. "The Hopes of Intercultural Education." *Social Science* 22, no. 1 (January 1947): 5–9.

Santos, R. Chris. "Doris 'Dorie' Miller." *Texas Historian* 37, no. 5 (May 1997): 10–12.

Sapper, Neil. "Aboard the Wrong Ship in the Right Books: Doris Miller and Historical Accuracy." *East Texas Historical Journal* 18, no. 1 (spring 1980): 3–11.

Web and Magazine Articles

Aiken, David. "Doris Miller and His Navy Cross: A Brief Biography." February 26, 2001. Pearl Harbor Message Board, http://www.pearlharborattacked .com/cgi-bin/IKONBOARDNEW312a/ikonboard.cgi?act=Print;f=20;t=15.

Allen, Thomas B. "Pearl Harbor: A Return to the Day of Infamy." *National Geographic Magazine*, December 1991, 50–77.

Binese, Henry L. "Negroes in the Navy." *Commonweal*, 21 September 1945, 546–48.

"Black Sailors." *Time*, 17 August 1942, 54.

Brooks, Gwendolyn. "Negro Hero—to Suggest Dorie Miller." *Common Ground* 5, no. 4 (summer 1945): 44–45.

Cagle, Jess. "Cinema: Pearl Harbor's Top Gun." *Time*, 4 June 2001, 69–72.

Calamur, Krishnadev. "Muhammad Ali and Vietnam." *The Atlantic*, 4 June 2016. https://www.theatlantic.com/news/archive/2016/06/muhammad-ali -vietnam/485717/.

Darden, Robert. "How Doris Miller Changed the Movies." http://www.doris-millermemorial.org/wp/wp-content/uploads/2012/11/How-Doris-Miller-Changed-the-Movies.pdf.

"Dorie Miller: First US Hero of World War II." *Ebony* 25, no. 2 (December 1969): 132–38.

Du Bois, W. E. B. "Close Ranks." *The Crisis*, no. 16 (July 1918): 111.

———. "Editorial." *The Crisis*, no. 16 (August 1918): 164.

———. "Returning Soldiers." *The Crisis*, no. 18 (May 1919): 13–14.

Grady, John. "Remembering an American Hero: Victor Delano." http://john-gradynowandthen.com/remembering-an-american-hero-victor-delano/.

Gregory, Trey. "Home of the Brave." *Baylor Focus Magazine* 32 (spring 2015): 32–34.

Joyner, MarshaRose. "Rethinking the Recognition of Doris Miller." *AFRO*, 26 March 2015, http://www.afro.com/rethinking-the-recognition-of-doris -miller/.

———. "The United States Navy Refuses to Acknowledge Its Racist Past," *AFRO*, 20 May 2015, http://www.afro.com/the-united-states-navy-refuses -to-acknowledge-its-racist-past/.

Kaderlik, R. J. "Haynes Survived Sinking of USS *Liscome Bay*," *Montrose Daily Press*, 2 August 2001. http://www.montrosepress.com/haynes-survived-sinking-of-uss-liscome-bay/article_c69c8835-6fd0-5e9a-897e9b e9d9f6a0a1.html.

Lanning, Wilton, Jr. "At Old Lake Waco, Meeting a Hero's Father." http://
    www.dorismillermemorial.org/wp/wp-content/uploads/2012/Doris-
    Miller-Lanning.pdf.
Mueller, William R. "The Negro in the Navy." *Social Forces* 24 (October 1945):
    110–15.
National Geographic. "Beyond the Movie: Pearl Harbor: Ship's Cook Third
    Class Doris 'Dorie' Miller." 2001. http://www.nationalgeographic.com/pearl
    harbor/ngbeyond/people/.
"Navy Honors Black Pearl Harbor Hero." *Jet*, 30 December 1971, 46–47.
"Navy Secretary Names Destroyer after Female Navy Cross Recipient." 14 June
    2016. http://www.military.com/daily-news/2016/06/14/navy-secretary-
    names-destroyer-after-female-navy-cross-recipient.html.
Perry, Harmon. "Navy Hero's Mother Bitter, Destitute, Despite Honors." *Jet*,
    1 December 1977, 44–47.
Schwartz, Robert L. "The Sinking of the *Liscome Bay*." *Yank*, 11 June 1944, 2–8;
    reprinted in Reprinted in *Yank: World War II from the Guys Who Brought
    You Victory*, edited by Steve Kluger, 123–29. New York: St. Martin's Press,
    1990.
Reagon, Bernice. "World War II Reflected in Black Music: 'Uncle Sam Called
    Me.'" *Southern Exposure* 1, nos. 3 and 4 (winter 1974): 170–84.
Tilove, Jonathan. "Six Decades after WWII's End, Dorie Miller's Faithful
    Fight for Medal of Honor." Newhouse News Service, 25 May 2004, https://
    jonathantilove.com/dorie-miller/.
Turner, Thomas E., Sr. "A Man Named Doris." *Texas Star* 2, no. 2 (21 May
    1972): 4–5.
————. "A Man Named Doris—Waco's Unlikely Hero." *Discover Waco* 2, no.
    4 (December 1991): 24–26.
"TV Networks Ignore Black Navy Hero Who Shot Down Japanese War Planes
    at Pearl Harbor." *Jet* 81, no. 10 (23 December 1991): 12–13.
Tygiel, Jules. "The Court-Martial of Jackie Robinson," *American Heritage Mag-
    azine* 35, no. 5 (August/September 1984): 34–39.
White, F. H. "Statement of Japanese Attack on December 7, 1941." 11 Decem-
    ber 1941, attached to R. H. Hillenkoetter to Commander-in-Chief, Pacific
    Fleet, "Action of December 7, 1941—Report of." http://www.usswestvirginia
    .org/white_statement.htm.

Newspaper Articles
"A Hero Returns; A Medal He Wears." *Pittsburgh Courier*, 19 December 1942,
    1.
Adams, Samuel. "From Squirrels to Bombers." *Waco Tribune-Herald*, 7 De-
    cember 1991, 1A, 10A.

Anderson, Mike. "Hero's Bravery Carved in Stone." *Waco Tribune-Herald*, 18 May 2003.

Bennett, James. "Medals of Honor Awarded at Last to Black World War II Soldiers." *New York Times*, 14 January 1997.

Booker, Bobbi. "From Messman to Pearl Harbor Hero." *Philadelphia Tribune*, 6 December 2011.

Burns, Eugene. "USS *Liscome Bay* Survivors Tell How Heroes Gave Lives to Save Shipmates." *Fort Worth Star-Telegram*, 14 December 1943.

Cansleb, J. O. "Nation Pays Tribute to Parent of Naval Hero." *Pittsburgh Courier*, 14 March 1942, 1.

Cantwell, Catherine. "Doris Miller Decorated 40 Years Ago." *Waco Tribune-Herald*, 3 May 1982.

Carter, Art. "U.S.S. Doris Miller Goes to Sea after Commissioning Ceremony." *Baltimore Afro-American*, 14 July 1973.

Copeland, Mike. "Doris Miller Stamp Presented in Waco before Packed House." *Waco Tribune-Herald*, 6 February 2010.

"Courier Campaigns for Return of Dorie." *Pittsburgh Courier*, 25 June 1942, 1.

"A Cross to Messman Miller." *New York Times*, 13 May 1942, 18.

"Dedicate Unbiased N.Y. Project." *Chicago Defender*, 26 December 1953.

"Dining Hall Named for Doris Miller." *Waco News-Tribune*, 4 June 1970.

"Dinner to Honor Texas Negro Who Won Navy Cross." *Dallas Morning News*, 2 January 1943, 7.

"Don't Give Up on Miller Medal." *Waco Tribune-Herald*, 27 May 1990.

"Dorie Miller, Hero at Pearl Harbor, Speaks." *Dallas Express*, 23 January 1943, 1.

"Dorie Miller Not in States, Navy Declares." *Pittsburgh Courier*, 23 May 1942, 1.

"Dorie Miller, Pearl Harbor Hero, First to Get Award." *Baltimore Afro-American*, 12 May 1945, 5.

"Dorie Miller Talks to Camp Smalls Grads." *Baltimore Afro-American*, January 16, 1943, 3.

"Dorie Miller Thrills Naval Graduating Class With Talk," *Pittsburgh Courier*, 16 January 1943, 1.

"Doris Miller: Hospital's Renaming Invites Us All to Ponder America's Past, Potential." *Waco Tribune-Herald*, 14 December 1994.

"Doris Miller's Medal Pinned." *Waco Times-Herald*, 28 May 1942, 1.

"Entire Navy Awarded Dorie Miller Trophy." *Baltimore Afro-American*, 14 October 1950, 1, 2.

"Film Depicts Texas Hero." *Austin American-Statesman*, 7 January 1971.

"First Bluejackets Finish; Addressed by Doris Miller." *Dallas Express*, 30 January 1943, 1.

Fountain, John W. "Black Navy Captain Is Honored," *Chicago Tribune*, 21 May 1990.

Hall, Douglass. "Man Who Saw Pearl Harbor Bombed Now D.C. Tailor." *Baltimore Afro-American*, 4 May 1943, 14.

Henderson, Nat. "Ship Named for Waco Hero." *Austin American-Statesman*, 2 July 1973.

"Honors Due for Waco Parents of Negro War Hero." *Waco Tribune-Herald*, 5 April 1942.

"I Had to Spank Doris to Make Him Protect Himself," *Pittsburgh Courier*, 14 May 1942, 4.

Johns, Pearl. "Dorie Miller Is Modest," *Baltimore Afro-American*, 17 April 1943, 1, 2.

Johnson, Eddie Bernice. "Honoring Dorie Miller." *Waco Tribune-Herald*, 15 June 2013.

Joseph, E. F. "'I Downed Four Enemy Planes'—Dory Miller." *Pittsburgh Courier*, 2 January 1943, 1.

Kinloch, John. "Back from Kiska, Dorie Rides in 'Dewdrop'—Lives." *California Eagle*, 7 October 1943, 1.

Lang, John. "Dorie Miller Was a Hero but the Navy Hasn't Caught On." Scripps Howard News Service, 15 January 1997.

Langer, Emily. "Santiago Erevia, Vietnam Veteran Who Belatedly Received the Medal of Honor, Dies at 70." *Washington Post*, 24 March 2016.

"The Late Unpleasantness." *Temple Daily Telegram*, 4 August 1915.

"Late Waco Hero's Mom Gets Help." *Austin America- Statesman*, 27 August 1974.

Levin, Steve. "Doris Miller's War for Recognition Is Still Being Fought." *Dallas Morning News*, 29 July 1990.

———. "For the Sailor's Honor" *Washington Post*, 14 July 1990.

———. "The Long War of Doris Miller." *Dallas Morning News*, 8 July 1990.

———. "Should Black Hero of Pearl Harbor Receive Medal of Honor?" *Dallas Morning News*, 25 July 1990.

Little, Linda. "Doris Miller Made Presence Felt." *Waco News-Tribune*, 28 January 1970.

"Messman Hero Identified." *Pittsburgh Courier*, 14 March 1942, 1.

"Movie May Detail Waco Man's Heroism at Pearl Harbor." *Austin American-Statesman*, 14 August 1990, B3.

"Mr. Knox Hasn't Said Enough, This Paper Still Believes in a Navy without Barriers." *Pittsburgh Courier*, 18 April 1942, 1.

"Mrs. Henrietta Miller" (obituary). *Waco Tribune-Herald*, 10 June 1982, 10D.

"Mrs. Miller Is Guest Speaker on 'Wings' Program over KTRH." *Dallas Express*, 16 May 1942, 1.

"Navy Bias Shaken by Mess Hero." *Pittsburgh Courier*, 3 September 1960.

"Navy Cross to Waco Negro as Heroism Award." *Waco Tribune-Herald*, 11 March 1942.

"Navy Naming Ship for Hero." *Austin American-Statesman*, 30 July 1971.

"Navy Pacific Hero Home on Furlough." *Pittsburgh Courier*, 2 January 1943, 2.

"Navy Transfers Ship Named for Wacoan." *Waco Tribune-Herald*, 24 January 1984.

"Negro Hero Reported Lost in Pacific Action." *Dallas Morning News*, 9 December 1943, 4.

"Negro Tells Students of Pearl Harbor Battle." *Dallas Morning News*, 21 January 1943, 6.

"New 20th Century-Fox Film to Touch Exploits of Dorie Miller." *Pittsburgh Courier*, 12 September 1942.

"97 Bluejackets Finish Great Lakes Training." *Pittsburgh Courier*, 30 January 1943, 24.

"No Time to Think, Says Negro Who Won Navy Cross." *Dallas Morning News*, 20 January 1943, 6.

"Presentation to Dorie Miller." *Pittsburgh Courier*, 2 January 1943, 19.

Ramsey, Leroy. "Medal of Honor," *Waco Tribune-Herald*, 21 August 1988.

"Remembering Pearl Harbor!" *Pittsburg Courier*, 8 December 1956.

Repko, Melissa. "Dallas Representative Eddie Bernice Johnson, Others Still Seek Medal of Honor for Pearl Harbor Hero 'Dorie' Miller." *Dallas Morning News*, 13 August 2015.

Rudner, Jordan, "Dorie Miller's Fans Keep Fighting to Honor Black Sailor's Pearl Harbor Heroism." *Dallas Morning News*, 7 December 2016.

Schapiro, Rich. "Black Sailor's Pearl Harbor Heroics Helped End Racism in Military." *New York Daily News*, 6 December 2016.

Schuyler, George S. "The World Today." *Pittsburgh Courier*, 6 February 1943, 1.

"7 Black World War II Vets Awarded Medal of Honor." *USA Today*, 14 January 1997.

Sheppard, Nathaniel, Jr. "Battle to Honor Blacks Pits Historian against Military." *Chicago Tribune*, 24 August 1988.

"Ship Honoring Dorie Miller Commissioned." *Pittsburgh Courier*, 21 July 1973.

Smith, J. B. "Austin Service Celebrates Doris Miller." *Waco Tribune-Herald*, 26 May 2001, 2B–3B.

———. "Valor at Sunrise: The Story of Pearl Harbor Hero Doris Miller." *Waco Tribune-Herald*, 20 May 2001, A1, A12.

Smith, Richard L. "Push for Doris Miller Medal Revived." *Waco Tribune-Herald*, 9 February 2005.

"Son Died in Vain, Says Dorie Miller's Father." *Baltimore Afro-American*, 15 December 1945, 1, 19.

Svendsen, Karen. "Wacoans Recall Hero's Bravery during Pearl Harbor Attack." *Waco Tribune-Herald*, 24 February 1984, 2B.

"Two-Race Navy Is Denounced by New York Racial Club." *Pittsburgh Courier*, 25 April 1942, 2.

"Varying Degrees of Opinion Greet New Naval Policy." *Pittsburgh Courier*, 18 April 1942, 1.

"Waco Pearl Harbor Hero Honored with Dedication of the Navy Quarters." *Waco News-Tribune*, 8 December 1971.

"Waco VA Center Renamed to Honor World War II Hero." *Waco Tribune-Herald*, 20 February 2015, 1A, 2A, 6A.

"Waco War Hero Honored Tuesday." *Waco Citizen*, 9 December 1971.

Walton, Amy. "The Mark of Heroism." *Waco Tribune-Herald*, 7 February 1994.

"We Are Americans, Too!" *Pittsburgh Courier*, 13 December 1941, 1.

"Willkie Championed Cause of Negro Americans." *Pittsburgh Courier*, 14 October 1944, 10.

"Willkie Pledges Aid in Fight to Return Dorie." *Pittsburgh Courier*, 11 July 1942, 4.

Government Documents

Harrod, Frederick S. "The Integration of the Navy (1941–1978)." *U.S. Naval Institute Proceedings* 105 (October 1979): 41–47.

President's Committee on Equality of Treatment and Opportunity in the Armed Services. *Freedom to Serve: Equality of Treatment and Opportunity in the Armed Services.* Washington, DC: US Government Printing Office, 1950.

US Naval War Records Office. *Official Records of the Union and Confederate Navies in the War of the Rebellion.* Washington, DC: Government Printing Office, 1894–1922.

Index

⟨⟩